D0559773

THE
TEA PARTY

Three Principles

ELIZABETH PRICE FOLEY

Florida International University College of Law

CAMBRIDGE UNIVERSITY PRESS
Cambridge, New York, Melbourne, Madrid, Cape Town,
Singapore, São Paulo, Delhi, Tokyo, Mexico City

Cambridge University Press
32 Avenue of the Americas, New York, NY 10013-2473, USA

www.cambridge.org
Information on this title: www.cambridge.org/9781107011359

First published 2012

Printed in the United States of America

A catalog record for this publication is available from the British Library.

Library of Congress Cataloging in Publication data
Foley, Elizabeth Price.
The Tea Party : three principles / Elizabeth Price Foley.
p.   cm.
Includes an index.
ISBN 978-1-107-01135-9 (hardback)
1. Tea Party movement.   I. Title.
JK2391.T43F65   2012
320.520973–dc23   2011040843

ISBN 978-1-107-01135-9 Hardback

To the intrepid members of the American Tea Party
movement, with admiration and respect

Contents

Preface

FOR MANY REASONS, THIS HAS BEEN THE MOST challenging book project I've ever undertaken. Nonetheless, it's been a labor of love. Writing a book about the Tea Party presents a unique set of challenges. For one reason or another, mere mention of the phrase "Tea Party" seems to incite passionate feelings from across the ideological spectrum. In many ways, Americans have come to love 'em or hate 'em; rarely does one encounter indifference. Because of this, telling someone you're writing a book "about the Tea Party" is often an awkward moment, engendering a pregnant pause during which one waits for the deluge of either effusive or suspicious comments. In an attempt to get along, I have found it generally more pleasant not to reveal my own thoughts about the Tea Party in the context of such conversations. Instead, I've learned to listen, soaking up the information conveyed and discerning the basis of the speaker's perspective.

This isn't to say that I don't have my own thoughts about the Tea Party. As the dedication to the book reveals, I've developed admiration and respect for the movement. This isn't a politically motivated conclusion: I consider myself libertarian, not pledging any particular allegiance to either the Republican or Democrat party. I am quite conservative on some issues, quite liberal on others.

But I haven't always been a libertarian, at least not in any overtly self-aware way. My journey to libertarianism has been a steady progression since I started law school many years ago. Before law school, I considered myself an ardent liberal, working on Capitol Hill as a policy adviser to several prominent Democrats. I fought vigorously for causes such as universal health care; expansion of Medicare and Medicaid; and greater regulation of insurance companies, food, drugs, and cosmetics.

The shocking thing, looking back on it all now, is how very little I actually knew about our government, despite the fact that I was knee-deep in its bowels, charged with the awesome responsibility of keeping high-ranking members of Congress advised on critical issues of the day. Although I considered myself well educated at the time, having attended a top-tier university, I had almost zero grasp of the Constitution or its foundational architectural features, such as federalism or limited power. Indeed, like most self-identified liberal well-educated Americans, if someone had told me then that the federal government – particularly Congress – lacked the power to accomplish a goal it deemed desirable for the public welfare, I would have laughed and dismissed the statement as right-wing, politically motivated lunacy.

My early ignorance of the Constitution wasn't unusual. In fact, it was normal. Most Americans – even college graduates – know shockingly little about their own Constitution. To be honest, the vast majority of lawyers don't know much more.

They read the assigned cases in the casebook, memorize the holdings, and don't really think much more about it.

The more one knows about the Constitution, however, the more one grows concerned, unless one thinks the Constitution has (and should have) no real fixed meaning. There is an incessant drumbeat in one's brain that says, "This is really important," "You need to know this," and "This country won't survive if you don't understand this." Realizing how much the founders studied and understood the intricacies of political philosophy and the science of government – and what high hopes they had for Americans to grasp these matters as well – creates an urgency about keeping their hopes from being extinguished.

It also, to a great extent, allows one to rise above petty politics. The modern labels "conservative" and "liberal" seem almost irrelevant in this context. What matters is preserving the Constitution, its meaning, and its foundational principles. All else is petty politics.

Unfortunately, however, many people just don't get this. Too often, very intelligent people view law – particularly constitutional law – as synonymous with politics. They view the Constitution through a political lens, embracing whatever interpretation serves their own political agenda. They consider anyone who disagrees with their own interpretation as equally politically motivated. It's almost as if they say, "You don't agree with me? Oh, you must be one of *them*." They cannot fathom that constitutional disagreement could be based on principles rather than politics.

With such a high degree of political polarization in modern America, it is challenging to teach constitutional law, to teach it objectively, and to write about it without being accused of belonging to this or that political camp. When the Tea Party burst onto the scene in 2009, I remember vividly thinking, "Wow. This could be a great opportunity." I wasn't thinking about a personal or political opportunity, I was thinking about an opportunity to educate people about the Constitution. It seemed to me then – and still does today – that the crises being experienced in America are creating both an angst and consequent curiosity about all things constitutional. Can Congress really make us buy health insurance? Can the president really commit troops to Libya, or try Guantánamo detainees in military tribunals? Can a state like Arizona really pass an immigration law like it did? These are all constitutional questions that, in one way or another, have been raised by the Tea Party movement.

There is admittedly no right or wrong way to interpret the Constitution. But we all form opinions about the best way to interpret it. My own preference is to interpret it with the goal of honoring its original meaning. If this proves unpalatable, there is a mechanism for change through the amendment process of Article V. In this sense, the Constitution has a stable fixed meaning, yet is subject to ultimate control and revision by each succeeding generation of We the People.

So yes, I am an originalist. But this doesn't make me automatically conservative, radical, or right wing. It doesn't make me a neocon. It doesn't even have anything to do with my position on particular issues, providing zero insight into my subjective preference on issues such as the war on terror, universal health care, abortion, or physician-assisted suicide. Originalism is an interpretive methodology with a principled basis. Like it or hate it, it isn't a Trojan horse for particular results – it's a neutral process for interpreting a complicated and often vague document. Living constitutionalism is likewise an interpretive methodology with a principled basis. I personally don't question this. I happen to think it's an inferior methodology for reasons I explain in the book – as does the Tea Party – but this doesn't mean I consider living constitutionalism to be an unprincipled position.

It is a commonality of principles that drives my admiration and respect for the Tea Party movement. Although most Tea Partiers never went to law school, they have a unique and intense desire to learn about, honor, and preserve the Constitution. I respect that. Although they don't always understand the finer nuances of constitutional doctrine, they know far more about the Constitution than average Americans – including college-educated Americans and a good deal of lawyers. They want to learn more about it; they seem hungry for information. I admire that. Their positions on most issues they've emphasized have a deep connection to the three constitutional principles discussed in the book. Recognizing this, as a constitutional law professor, I feel well positioned to write about the Tea Party from a perspective that focuses exclusively on these constitutional principles.

It's important to understand what this book is not about. It's not a book about policy or politics. I'm not a professor of political science or policy. I teach constitutional law, so this book has tried to maintain a laser-beam focus on the constitutional principles I see as unifying the Tea Party movement. Specifically, the book examines the Tea Party's position on various key modern issues, examining them through the lens of three core constitutional principles. It explains what those principles mean and why it may be important to preserve those principles, even when politically inexpedient.

I have assiduously tried to avoid being distracted from these principles by getting bogged down in a discussion of their impact on particular desired policy outcomes or their political wisdom. In the discussion preserving U.S. sovereignty, for example, I haven't discussed President Obama's decision to order the assassination of Osama bin Laden for the simple reason that the Tea Party hasn't voiced any particular criticism of this decision. The movement's failure to condemn the president's decision is understandable, as it certainly isn't antithetical to the principle of U.S. sovereignty. So my failure to discuss some issues isn't an attempt to downplay good policy or political decisions made by the president. If a decision implicates one of these three principles, I have endeavored to discuss it fully and accurately.

Similarly, I don't spend time discussing the Tea Party's position on the armed conflicts in Afghanistan or Iraq, because the movement doesn't seem to have a unified position on them. When the Tea Party has expressed concern about the use of military force – for example, President Obama's decision to commit U.S. military forces to the Libyan conflict – it is motivated by its concerns about pandering to globalists and the United Nations, concerns that do implicate the principle of U.S. sovereignty.

To make this point about constitutional principles, I've found it necessary to debunk the false portrayals of the Tea Party movement. Hard as some may try, I don't think it's accurate to portray Tea Partiers as motivated by politics, hatred of President Obama, or racism. If one understands the Constitution well, it's apparent that the movement's primary motivation is grounded in these three principles. Whether one agrees with the Tea Party's embrace or interpretation of these constitutional principles, an honest and educated assessment of their statements and positions reveals an elevation of principles over politics.

It's similarly important to realize that, although I do identify three unifying constitutional principles that underlie the movement's position on various issues, I'm not suggesting that these are the only principles or issues of interest to Tea Partiers. The Tea Party is a vast, dispersed, grassroots movement. There is no central leader, organization, or even organizing committee. There are small chapters scattered throughout the country, with rough coordination via social media, the Internet, and local activist groups. Yet this apparent disorganization doesn't mean there's no identifiable or coherent Tea Party movement. As I point out in the book, it's fair to say there's no Tea *Party*, but there is a Tea Party movement. The emphasis must be on the movement rather than the party because Tea Partiers seem to have no interest in forming an independent third political party, but instead have opportunistically infiltrated existing political parties (mostly the Republican Party), pressuring them to embrace principles of importance to the movement. So although some may object that there is no unified Tea Party, I respectfully disagree; there's admittedly no party, but there is a clearly identifiable set of principles that permeate and ultimately define the movement.

Some claim that the Tea Party is essentially indistinguishable from the Republican Party and indeed is the brainchild of clever conservative and/or libertarian organizations and thus is essentially captured by them. Although there are admittedly conservative and libertarian organizations (and the two are not the same, by the way) that support and are sympathetic to the Tea Party movement, it would be unfair to characterize the Tea Party as a mere spin-off of such organizations or a puppet of them. In my opinion, it's quite the contrary: Tea Partiers have, on many occasions, not backed establishment

Republican candidates, preferring instead to support dark-horse candidates who are more closely aligned with their position on various issues. The movement has shown a ruthless ability to reject any candidate, of any party, who doesn't embrace their principles and a persistence in pursuing their agenda with any candidate who'll listen. To the extent that the Tea Party has been more successful in obtaining the ear of the Republican Party, this suggests that the Republican Party may be (or is becoming) accountable to the Tea Party, not vice versa.

With all of these prefatory explanations out of the way, I ask you to open your mind and explore three foundational principles embraced by the Tea Party: (1) limited government, (2) unapologetic U.S. sovereignty, and (3) constitutional originalism. Whether you like the Tea Party or not, I hope by the time you finish reading this book, you will agree that the primary motivation of the movement is its desire to preserve these three principles. This perspective may allow you to make a better-informed judgment about the movement, its motivations, and the need to engage in a productive dialogue about the continuing salience of these constitutional principles.

Acknowledgments

WRITING A BOOK WITH POLITICAL OVERTONES is never easy. There is always the chance that someone will misconstrue something you say, take it out of context, or simply misunderstand the purpose of writing. It becomes critically important, therefore, to get an honest assessment of the strengths and weaknesses from colleagues, family members, and anonymous reviewers. Although having such feedback cannot guarantee that such problems can be avoided, it can minimize them and, in the end, makes for a stronger, although no less passionate, book.

I have been very fortunate to have such honest assessment from many people while writing this book. First and foremost, I have had the benefit of an experienced and objective editor, Robert Dreesen, who has not been afraid to share with me the good, bad, and ugly along the way. He has done so with grace, wisdom, and unflagging enthusiasm for the project. Thanks also to the anonymous reviewers who offered both praise and constructive criticism. Their comments have made a stronger book. I have also been blessed to have had sage advice from several people whom I greatly admire and trust, including

Randy Barnett, Chip Mellor, David Rivkin, and George Will. Without their encouragement and support, I probably would have given up somewhere along the way.

The able and accurate research assistance of Robert Scavone has been invaluable. His ability to find polling data and obscure nonlegal sources is nothing short of amazing.

Last but not least, I want to thank my husband, Patrick, and daughter, Kate, for being the best family a girl could ever hope for. They never complain when I spend hours hunched over a computer or spread skyscraper-sized stacks of research papers across various rooms of the house. They are a constant source of cheerfulness, love, faith, and security – precious commodities always, but particularly so when one is overworked, overcommitted, or overwhelmed. I could not do what I do without them, and I simply cannot thank them enough.

☆ I ☆

Genesis

W HAT MAKES AMERICA, AMERICA? IS ITS ROLE in the world unique, or is it just another country? Is there anything to the idea of American exceptionalism? What role does the U.S. Constitution play in answering these questions? The genesis of the American Tea Party is rooted in a growing angst over these questions, and this book suggests that the movement is defined by unified answers to them.

In recent decades, the notion of American exceptionalism has become politically incorrect. Critics assert that America should embrace the larger global community and stop being so standoffish. They characterize those who advocate exceptionalism as jingoistic, xenophobic, myopic, and hell bent on imperialism. The antiexceptionalists denounce the U.S. military interventions in Iraq and Afghanistan, decry attempts to protect American borders as racist, and condemn the founding fathers as irrelevant and backward thinking.

Rejecting, and even mocking, American exceptionalism has become a favorite pastime of some on the political left. Rather than being a beacon of hope and model of success for the world to emulate, America is often portrayed as a sinful hypocrite, marred by a history of military interventionism, economic inequality, slavery, and segregation. They see the current war on terror as a self-imposed consequence of arrogant, imperialistic U.S. foreign policy. For example, Michael Scheuer, a former intelligence officer with the Central Intelligence Agency, has asserted that "the current anger of everyday Americans should actually be directed at themselves. They, after all, have elected the last four interventionist presidents who have waged what most Muslims perceive as a cultural, military, and foreign-policy war against Islam meant to remake Muslims in contemporary America's militantly secular image."

Damon Linker's essay in the *New Republic* similarly asserted that America is at best a work in progress, not anything "exceptional" worth bragging about: "[I]t is most certainly not the case . . . that America's creed of liberty – including the principle of equality and respect – was 'open to all' from the beginning. On the contrary, it was closed to many until quite recently." Linker equates American exceptionalism with moral superiority and ultimately confesses that "liberal love for the United States is complicated by criticism." Michael Kinsley has been even brasher in his disparagement, asserting, "The important message of this election [the 2010 midterm election] is not from the voters but to the voters. Maybe it can be heard above the din. It is: You're not so special. The notion that America and Americans are special, among all the peoples of the earth, is sometimes called 'American exceptionalism.' . . . [It means] the rules don't apply to us. There are man-made rules like, 'You can't start a war without the permission of the United Nations Security Council.' We've gotten away with quite a bit of bending or breaking of that kind of rule.... No country is special enough to escape these rules."

It is tempting to dismiss such statements as the rantings of a political fringe, but unfortunately, the Obama administration shares their views. In a now-famous interview with a *Financial Times* reporter during his first official overseas trip, President Obama was asked whether he subscribes "to the school of American exceptionalism that sees America as uniquely qualified to lead the world," to which he replied, "I believe in American exceptionalism, just as I suspect that the Brits believe in British exceptionalism and the Greeks believe in Greek exceptionalism." The president's idea of exceptionalism, in other words, was a type of narcissism possessed by all countries. If every country is equally entitled to believe it's exceptional, then none is really exceptional, just self-centered.

Subsequent statements by the Obama administration have confirmed this Orwellian double-speak concept of unexceptional exceptionalism. In a recent report to the UN Human Rights Commission, for example, the Obama administration declared, "The story of the United States is one guided by universal values shared the world over – that all are created equal and endowed with inalienable rights.... Our founders, who proclaimed their ambition 'to form a more perfect union,' bequeathed to us not a static condition but a perpetual aspiration and mission." If you read the passage carefully, the message of unexceptional exceptionalism is inescapable: although the United States was founded on values like equality and individual rights, those values are universal, not uniquely American, and more important, America hasn't yet fully realized them. The tone is one of "we're just like everybody else" and "if only we could live up to these worthy aspirations."

If there was any doubt about the political left's embrace of unexceptional exceptionalism, the Obama administration's report to the Human Rights Commission made it clear, declaring: "Although we have made great strides, work remains to meet our goal of ensuring equality before the law.... Indeed, our nation's struggle to banish the legacy of slavery and our long and continuing journey toward racial equality have become the central and emblematic narrative in our quest for a fair and just society that reflects the equality of all." The report suggests that racial disparities in employment, home ownership, college degrees, and even health status are the result of continuing racial discrimination in America. The report also atoned for the Constitution's "original flaw of tolerating slavery, as well as denying the vote to women," for the fact that "[w]hen the United States was founded, only white men who owned property could vote," for "past wrongs and broken promises in the federal government's relationship with American Indians and Alaska Natives," for "linguistic discrimination," and for "concerns about our nation's criminal justice system . . . including in the areas of capital punishment, juvenile justice, racial profiling, and racial disparities in sentencing."

The Obama administration's habit of apologizing for perceived U.S. sins – particularly when traveling abroad – has become so commonplace that media outlets and pundits dubbed a recent sojourn an "apology tour." In April 2009, while in Strasbourg, France, the president declared that "there have been times where America has shown arrogance and been dismissive, even derisive" to Europe. While speaking at the Summit of the Americas in Trinidad and Tobago in the same month, the president told world leaders that the United States "at times [has] been disengaged and . . . sought to dictate our terms." He told the Turkish Parliament that the United States "is still working through some of our own darker periods in history.... Our country still struggles with the legacy of slavery and segregation, the past treatment of Native Americans." And speaking before a domestic audience at the National Archives, President Obama atoned for the sin of operating a detention facility at Guantánamo Bay, Cuba – a facility he promised to close – because it "undermined the rule of law" and was intentionally located outside U.S. soil to "be beyond the law."

As President Obama's statements illustrate, many of the political left don't understand why America can't be more humble and less hegemonic, adopting European-style social democratic norms such as disarmament, binding global adjudication, nationalized health care, fluorescent light bulbs, and tiny cars. But such an American role reversal would come at a high price. To implement this progressive new world order, America would need to relinquish its role as world superpower. After all, one cannot simultaneously be a coequal participant in global governance and paternalistic protector of worldwide democracy. To join the club, in other words, the United States cannot seek to dominate or even lead it.

In a speech in Cairo in the summer of 2009, for example, President Obama revealed his understanding of the consequences of a new world order, proclaiming, "Given our interdependence, any world order that elevates one nation or group of people over another will inevitably fail. So whatever we think of the past, we must not be prisoners to it. Our problems must be dealt with through partnership; our progress must be shared." With regard to the specific consequences for U.S. military might, President Obama told the predominantly Muslim Cairo audience that the U.S. action in Iraq could not be justified in the name of democracy building, saying, "So let me be clear: No system of government can or should be imposed by one nation by any other." More shocking, President Obama told the Cairo crowd, "I understand those who protest that some countries have weapons that others do not. No single nation should pick and choose which nation holds nuclear weapons."

President Obama's message couldn't be any clearer: The United States has been a powerful bully in the past, but under his leadership, it will no longer seek to impose its values – including democracy – on the rest of the world. In this worldview, the only exceptionalism to which the United States can rightly lay claim is a history of exceptional arrogance and aggression. This certainly isn't the kind of exceptionalism espoused by prior presidents or understood by average Americans. More important, if the United States isn't willing to play the role of chief promoter and defender of democracy – as it did in World War I, World War II, and the Cold War – who will?

Although moral superiority is perhaps unwarranted, Americans – particularly the president – both can and should be proud of their country, not embarrassed by it. It is this resurgent pride of the American people – a backlash against the antiexceptionalism of the modern progressive movement – that has given rise to the Tea Party movement. Tea Partiers are united in their belief that America is exceptional, in the sense of having a legal and governmental structure that is unique and worth preserving and promoting. Indeed, much of the current U.S. political divide centers on this difference of agreement about what *exceptionalism* means: does it mean that the United States is "better" than the rest of the world, or just different in a way that is worth preserving and defending? The political left defines exceptionalism as the former; the political right (including the Tea Party) as the latter.

Members of the Tea Party consider exceptionalism to be shorthand for defending foundational American principles against a culture of political correctness that has openly declared war on them. By October 2010, a Rasmussen poll revealed that 74 percent of Americans believed that political correctness was a problem for the country. And a February 2011 Rasmussen poll showed that almost two-thirds of Americans – 64 percent – think America is heading down the "wrong track." Tea partiers undoubtedly fall into this camp, united in their fearless query, "What happened to the America I grew up in?" Equally important, they advocate decidedly reembracing these "old-fashioned" American principles.

The growing perception that America's foundational principles are on the verge of a deep, dark, politically correct precipice has created a political environment akin to a gas leak. It was only a matter of time before something ignited the flames of political resistance. As it turned out, the spark was a free-falling economy and a crumbling housing market. For years, Wall Street greed and congressional policies combined to encourage widespread departure from traditional mortgage lending practices, in which no-documentation, no-money-down, interest-only, high debt-to-income-ratio, and other high-risk or "subprime" loans became commonplace.

In late 2008, in the waning days of George W. Bush's presidency, the full toxicity of these risky lending practices finally became apparent. Banks that had initiated the risky mortgages were eager to shift the risk onto others. Thanks to the quasi-government agencies Fannie Mae and Freddie Mac, banks could sell these risky mortgages to the government, which then pooled them with other mortgages and sold them to investors as mortgage-backed securities. When the economy and housing prices began sliding backward in 2006, these pooled mortgage investments plummeted in value. Because some of the country's – indeed, the world's – largest institutional investors, such as corporations and pension funds, had invested heavily in these mortgage-backed securities, the economic downturn affected not only individuals who defaulted on their mortgages but also the national and global economies. The whole house of cards came tumbling down.

The unholy alliance between lenders and the government culminated in the Troubled Asset Relief Program (TARP), an unprecedented $700 billion federal bailout that shored up big banks supposedly "too big to fail." The TARP money also bailed out the domestic auto industry to the tune of almost $11,000 for every GM and Chrysler car sold through the end of 2010. But although TARP was unprecedented, it turned out to be far from isolated. Taxpayers were also forced to foot an almost $500 billion federal takeover of smaller banks and a $430 billion bailout extending unemployment insurance, infusing pension funds, and bankrolling a cash-for-clunkers program. Congress also decided to rescue the agencies responsible for encouraging and insuring all the toxic mortgages – Fannie Mae and Freddie Mac – by authorizing the U.S. Treasury to purchase their stock for up to $400 billion.

As if this weren't enough spending, a second massive stimulus plan – the 2009 American Recovery and Reinvestment Act (ARRA) – doled out more than $820 billion dollars for tax credits (e.g., the first-time-homebuyer tax credit), infrastructure projects, additional expansion of unemployment and food stamp benefits, subsidies for continuation of health insurance for the unemployed, and funds shoring up state

Medicaid and education programs. Because some of the ARRA's provisions were initially temporary, Congress subsequently opted to enact a separate, more than $250 billion extension of these massive entitlements, keeping federal dollars flowing for many more months. Unemployment benefits, for example, were ultimately expanded to an astounding ninety-nine weeks.

The federal government's shift into bailout mode appeared unending, reflecting the resurgence of a Keynesian economic philosophy in which a failing economy can best be salvaged by a constant infusion of government cash – a counterintuitive, let's spend-our-way-out-of-this-mess mentality. The American public was told by both Presidents Bush and Obama that such massive spending was necessary to avoid another Great Depression. Given the unpalatable choice between depression and massive new debt, Americans chose the latter, albeit reluctantly. But Americans' acquiescence to this approach steadily eroded as economic indicators not only failed to rebound but also worsened. President Obama assured the American public that, with the passage of the ARRA, unemployment would be kept to 8 percent or less. Yet after the ARRA's enactment, the jobless rate continued to hover above 9 percent, reaching 9.8 percent by November 2010.

Adding insult to an already-injured economy, the Obama administration forged ahead on its proposal to remake the American health-care system, introducing a bill costing nearly a trillion dollars. From the beginning, the numbers just didn't add up: Americans were supposed to believe that 32 million people would gain access to health care without costing the federal government a dime, and it would magically reduce the deficit by $138 billion.

In *Alice in Wonderland* style, the health-reform numbers became curiouser and curiouser, as accounting gimmicks used to support the deficit reduction claim were brought to light. Significantly, the costs of expanding health-care access were hidden by simply mandating that everyone buy health insurance and that employers' subsidize low- to moderate-income employees' premiums. The net result was that the real cost of health reform was shifted entirely off the government's books and onto the backs of individuals and businesses.

In addition, the final reform law did not contain a $300 billion "doc fix" relieving physicians of a major cut in Medicare reimbursements. The multibillion-dollar price tag of this necessary fix was ignored when calculating health reform's official cost estimates, although everyone in Washington knew such a fix would have to be passed in a separate bill. The health-reform law cost estimate also relied on revenues that are unlikely to ever be realized, including $500 billion in projected future Medicare spending cuts and $149 billion in new taxes for "Cadillac" health insurance plans (not slated to go into effect until 2018). Both of these large revenue raisers are widely perceived as so unpopular and disruptive that Congress will never allow them to be fully implemented, thus rendering them little more than smoke and mirrors.

Once the basic parameters of health reform became known in the summer of 2009, Tea Partiers' anger about it – and the vision of bloated government it represented – erupted into large, vocal protests at congressional members' August town-hall meetings. Protesters chanted "Kill the Bill!," asked their representatives if they had read the 2,700-plus page proposal, and pointedly challenged them to cite the constitutional power source allowing Congress to force citizens to buy health insurance.

In reaction, Democratic Speaker of the House Nancy Pelosi and Majority Leader Steny Hoyer wrote an op-ed for *USA Today*, accusing the town-hall protesters of acting in a manner that was "simply un-American." *New York Times* columnist Paul Krugman declared that "cultural and racial anxiety" of "angry white voter[s]" was the "driving force behind the town hall mobs." Echoing this sentiment, a remarkable essay in *Psychology Today* by the psychologist Stephen Diamond asserted that the town-hall protests were the manifestation of a condition called posttraumatic embitterment disorder (PTED), a psychological disorder marked by "chronic feelings of injustice, victimhood, helplessness, hopelessness, powerlessness, self-recrimination, aggression, anger, rage, resentment and, of course, embitterment." Diamond explained that PTED is triggered when "individuals feel they have lost control of their lives and their destiny. The values and structure that once provided a stable sense of self, meaning, purpose and personal or professional identity been lost or eroded." Although the description of what Tea Partiers feel may be somewhat accurate – feelings of hopelessness, powerlessness, anger – Diamond not only insinuates that Tea Partiers are psychologically disturbed but also proclaims, "The anger, resentment and hostility I refer to here is also raising its ugly head in the form of racial hatred." In other words, Americans who protest against health-care reform and other Obama administration policies aren't doing so because of substantive disagreements about policy; they're doing so because the president is black.

This incessant, pull-out-the-race-card response to any and all opposition to the Obama administration's policies only exacerbates the anger and sense of frustration that Tea Partiers feel. It is a vicious circle of anger-racial accusation-anger that is escalating and deepening the ideological division in this country. Obamacare just happens to have become the fulcrum of this division.

Polls have revealed this ideological division and health care's centrality to it, with a majority of Americans consistently opposing health-care reform. Despite this opposition, a Democratic-dominated Congress passed health reform anyway by narrow, overwhelmingly partisan majorities, by employing controversial parliamentary procedures. The most unpopular provisions of the law – such as the individual mandate – were not slated to take effect until 2014, several years after enactment, and well after the intervening 2010 midterm and 2012 presidential elections. The not-so-subtle political calculation of Obamacare supporters was that, once the American public "got used to" the law – after the initial political shock and furor died down – they would either embrace it or at least become manageably indifferent.

But the furor over Obamacare didn't die down. Almost a year after congressional enactment, a late July 2011 Rasmussen poll revealed that 57 percent of Americans favored repealing the health-care overhaul. Exit polls from the November 2010 midterm elections showed that voters ranked health care as the second most important issue, trailing only the economy. As a result of this continuing and widespread opposition to health-care reform, the Republican Party, which had courted the Tea Party vote, took back control of the House of Representatives and gained six seats in the U.S. Senate.

Beyond this important legislative shift – which undoubtedly will affect Obamacare's funding and implementation – health-reform opponents have also sought relief from the judicial branch. Minutes after Obamacare was signed into law, a group of states, led by Florida Attorney General Bill McCollum, filed a lawsuit in federal court, claiming that the law was unconstitutional. Other states and affected groups quickly followed suit, initiating litigation in courts throughout the country. The Florida lawsuit has remained the most important case, expanding to garner support from the majority of states – an astonishing and unprecedented statement about the breadth and depth of opposition to Obamacare.

The constitutional litigation against Obamacare has centered on two primary contentions. First, they highlight Obamacare's negative impact on individual liberty. The reform law's so-called individual mandate requires that those without government-sponsored health care – such as Medicare or Medicaid – buy a private health insurance policy satisfying minimum federal standards. Individuals who fail to do so have to pay a hefty fine. The Obama administration claims the individual mandate is constitutionally permitted under a portion of the Constitution that grants Congress the power to regulate interstate commerce. But does the power to regulate interstate commerce include the power to force citizens to buy private products? If it does, couldn't Congress force individuals to buy other products, too – such as cars, shoes, or vegetables? The potential implications for individual liberty are enormous.

Second, the lawsuits challenging Obamacare focus on federalism – that is, the vertical separation of powers between the federal and state governments. Because the United States is not a monolithic national government but a federal one – in which sovereignty is split up among the federal government, the state governments, and the people – it has been a foundational principle of American law that the federal government cannot do whatever it wants, but can exercise only the limited and enumerated powers specified in the Constitution. This is the unmistakable message of the Tenth Amendment, which declares, "The powers not delegated to the United States by the Constitution, nor prohibited by it to the States, are reserved to the States respectively, or to the people." The question posed by Obamacare, therefore, was whether provisions vastly expanding Medicaid – a health program for the poor that is financed jointly by the state and federal governments – violates states' rights by effectively forcing them to spend billions of dollars they can't afford.

As you can see from these two arguments against Obamacare, the fear is that, although the end goal of expanding access may be laudable, the means used to achieve this goal represent a departure from prior understandings about the limits of federal power. And if sustained by the courts, Obamacare could have potentially far-reaching consequences for both individual liberty and states' rights.

When the potential effects of Obamacare were combined with the massive bailouts that expanded the federal government's tentacles into large swaths of the banking, finance, housing, and automobile industries, concern about the direction of the country reached a fever pitch. Americans began to wonder: Are these actions constitutional? Does the federal government really have this much power? And, pragmatically, how are we going to pay for all of this? What will it do to our children and grandchildren, and who will ultimately bear the brunt of the costs? How will these measures affect the value of the U.S. dollar and America's position as the world's leader?

The feelings of frustration and discontent boiled over on February 19, 2009, when CNBC reporter Rick Santelli stood on the floor of the Chicago Mercantile Exchange, unable to hold back his feelings any longer, and asserted, "the government is promoting bad behavior" by "subsidiz[ing] the losers' mortgages." When the traders behind Santelli erupted in cheers of support, a CNBC colleague quipped, "It's like mob rule here, I'm getting scared." Santelli responded, "Don't get scared, Joe. They're [government] already scaring you. . . . We're thinking of having a Chicago Tea Party in July. All you capitalists that want to show up to Lake Michigan, I'm going to start organizing. . . . We're going to be dumping in some derivative [mortgage-backed] securities. What do you think about that?" A CNBC in-studio guest then responded, "Rick, I congratulate you on your new incarnation as a revolutionary leader," to which Santelli replied, "Somebody needs one. I'll tell you what: if you read our Founding Fathers, people like Benjamin Franklin and Jefferson, what we're doing in this country now is making them roll over in their graves."

With Santelli's simple, frank comments, the Tea Party movement was officially born. Fewer than two months after Santelli's statements, on tax day in 2009, hundreds of thousands of Americans attended the first official "tea parties" across the country, ranging from small get-togethers in homes to large-scale rallies in the streets. By the fall of 2010, with the help of radio talk-show host Glenn Beck and various Tea Party groups, a so-called 9/12 rally was held on the mall in Washington, D.C., drawing hundreds of thousands of people. Participants held signs protesting the Obama administration's policies, declaring, "I am not your ATM," "Don't stimulate, liberate," "What would Jefferson do?" and "I'm taking back my country, one politician at a time."

The Tea Party movement is proving to be powerful, peaceful, and persistent. Tea Partiers have met with an unprecedented degree of skepticism and hostility from left-leaning media outlets, whose pundits and reporters have pejoratively (and crudely) labeled them as tea baggers, anarchists, neo-Nazis, and right-wing nut jobs. They have been consistently portrayed as "incredibly, earth shatteringly stupid" racists who are unknowing dupes of manipulative conservative billionaires and corporate America. A recent *Rolling Stone* diatribe by Matt Taibbi, for example, concluded that the movement was the brainchild of the Republican Party, which cobbled together "an assortment of nativist freaks, village idiots and Internet Hitlers" who collectively comprise a "giant ball of incoherent resentment." The resentment is supposedly aimed at the fact that the "country is becoming more black and more Hispanic by the day" and an "appalling horseshit fantasy about how white people in the age of Obama are some kind of oppressed minority." Similarly, MSNBC host Keith Olbermann called the Tea Party the "Tea Klux Klan" and declared that their anger is because "the president is black. But you can't come out and say that's why you're scared." Olbermann's evidence? In his words, "[L]et me ask all of you who attend these [Tea Party] things: How many black faces do you see at these events? How many Hispanics? Asians? Gays? Where are these people?"

Polling data does not confirm such demographically lop-sided portrayals of those who support the Tea Party movement. An April 2010 poll by *USA Today* and Gallup found that in "their age, educational background, employment status, and race – Tea Partiers are quite representative of the public at large." Tea Partiers are slightly more male than the general population (55 percent versus 49 percent), slightly better off economically (55 percent versus 50 percent make more than $50,000), and much less likely to call themselves liberal than the general population (7 percent versus 21 percent).

Racially, Tea Partiers have virtually the same proportion of non-Hispanic whites as the general population (79 percent versus 75 percent) and the exact same proportion of Hispanic and other races (15 percent). When it comes to African Americans, however, the Tea Party does have a definite disadvantage, with only 6 percent of its supporters self-identifying as black, versus 11 percent of the general population. This difference shouldn't be surprising, given Tea Partiers' high self-identification as conservative versus the general population (70 percent versus 40 percent) and low self-identification as Democrat (8 percent versus 32 percent). By contrast, black support for President Obama – the first president to self-identify as African American – is overwhelming. Ninety-five percent of blacks voted for Obama during the 2008 presidential election. And as of February 2011, a Gallup poll revealed that 93 percent of blacks still gave the president a favorable approval rating, compared with 40 percent of white and 55 percent of Hispanic voters.

Of course none of this is to say that the Tea Party lacks minority support or participation. It just means that, compared to the Democratic Party, the Tea Party's relative conservatism – much as the Republican Party's – is unlikely to resonate broadly in the black community. Yet the Tea Party movement has thrown its support behind many successful minority candidates, including Governors Susana Martinez of New Mexico and Nikki Haley of South Carolina; U.S. Senator Marco Rubio of Florida; and U.S. Representatives Allen West of Florida, Tim Scott of South Carolina, and Bill Flores and Francisco "Quico" Canseco of Texas.

Although most polls show that there are slightly more male than female Tea Party supporters (55 versus 45 percent, according to an April 2010 *USA Today*/Gallup poll), it would be foolish to underestimate the impact of women on the Tea Party movement. In addition to successful gubernatorial candidates Susana Martinez and Nikki Haley, Sharon Angle in Nevada and Christine O'Donnell in Delaware were ultimately unsuccessful in their bids for U.S. Senate but along the way garnered national attention and wielded significant influence. Congresswoman Michele Bachmann of Minnesota is a popular and outspoken advocate of the Tea Party movement and is founder of the congressional Tea Party Caucus. Sarah Palin, the former governor of Alaska and vice presidential running mate of John McCain in 2008, articulated the centrality of women to the Tea Party movement in her now-famous "mama grizzlies" video, declaring:

> [A] a lot of women, who are very concerned about their kids' future, are saying, "We don't like this fundamental transformation and we're going to do something about it!" . . . I always think of the mamma grizzly bears who always rise up on their hind legs when somebody is coming to attack their cubs. . . . And that's what we are seeing with all these women who are banding together rising up, saying, "No, this isn't right for our kids and for grandkids and we are going to do something about this. We are going to turn this thing around, we're going to get our country back on the right track."

These mama grizzlies not only have been involved in the Tea Party movement from the beginning but also have employed technologically sophisticated means, including Facebook, Twitter, and blogs, to organize and spread the word about grassroots Tea Party events. Most of them had never been politically involved before.

So why are so many women attracted to the Tea Party? Maybe it's because women are often responsible for balancing their own family budgets, or because they don't want their own children and grandchildren saddled with debt, or simply because they disagree with Keynesian economic philosophy. Whatever the reason, it seems clear that the self-styled mama grizzlies and "mommy" bloggers have come to constitute a critically important component of the Tea Party movement.

Given the wide range of demographic characteristics of those who self-identify as part of the Tea Party movement, what, if anything, binds this group together? Although there are certainly a wide range of issues important to the Tea Party groups scattered across the country, there appear to be three core principles shared by all of them, which are unique and essential to American identity: (1) limited government – protecting and defending the idea that the federal government possesses only those powers enumerated in the Constitution; (2) unapologetic U.S. sovereignty – protecting and defending America's borders and independent position in the world; and (3) constitutional originalism – interpreting the Constitution in a manner consistent with the meaning ascribed by those who wrote and ratified the text. These three core principles are reflected in a variety of current issues of importance to the Tea Party, including health-care reform, fiscal responsibility, immigration, internationalism, and the war on terror. This book examines the intellectual foundations of these three core principles, their role in current issues, and the reasons Tea Partiers consider them so important.

☆ 2 ☆

Limited Government

Much of the Constitution is concerned with setting forth the form of our government, and the courts have traditionally invalidated measures deviating from that form. The result may appear "formalistic" in a given case to partisans of the measure at issue, because such measures are typically the product of the era's perceived necessity. But the Constitution protects us from our own best intentions: It divides power among sovereigns and among branches of government precisely so that we may resist the temptation to concentrate power in one location as an expedient solution to the crisis of the day.

– *New York v. United States* (1992)

THE DOMINANT THEME OF THE TEA PARTY MOVEMENT IS its insistence on limited government. In the words of the movement's Contract from America, the movement seeks to "restore limited government consistent with the U.S. Constitution's meaning." The most prominent examples of this principle are the Tea Party's opposition to bailouts and health-care reform, although it is also evident in the movement's support of things like a rule requiring congressional bills to cite their constitutional power source and proposed constitutional amendments to require a balanced budget, to restore federalism, and to permit states to veto federal laws.

But what does limited government really mean, and why is it so important to the Tea Party? The idea comes from the Constitution itself and its unique concept of a government that possesses only limited and enumerated powers. The federal government – contrary to popular understanding – doesn't have the power to do whatever it wants, whenever it wants. It can exercise only those powers enumerated in the Constitution. This is the essence of limited government.

The founding generation rebelled against a form of government that wielded unlimited power. The king – and later Parliament – could do no wrong. This kind of omnipotent government, described and defended by Thomas Hobbes in *The Leviathan*, was something the founders rejected completely, spilling their blood to resist. Their alternative vision, articulated most forcefully by the English philosopher John Locke, was that government should be based not on force but on the consent of the people, who were born with inalienable natural rights – meaning rights that couldn't legitimately be taken away by government. In the words of the Declaration of Independence, "We hold these truths to be self evident, that all men are created equal, that they are endowed by their Creator with certain unalienable Rights, that among these are Life, Liberty, and the pursuit of Happiness. – That to secure these rights, governments are instituted among Men, deriving their just powers from the consent of the governed."

Under this radically new vision, government had only those powers explicitly ceded by the people. There was no all-powerful Leviathan; in its place, our founders created a government by the people, for the people. The blueprint for this novel form of government was the Constitution.

The newly created national government needed to mesh with thirteen preexisting state governments. For various reasons, the founders didn't have any desire to abolish the state governments or turn them into subsidiaries of the new national government. Instead, they acknowledged that there were many things best handled locally and a few specific things for which a uniform national approach seemed better. The Constitution explicitly granted the national government power in these latter areas, enumerating a laundry list of limited powers for which uniformity was important – things like coining money, regulating interstate and foreign commerce, declaring war, and raising and supporting an army. In all other areas, in the words of the Tenth Amendment, power was "reserved to the States respectively, or to the people."

So although the preexisting states needed to "unite" to form a "more perfect union," their unification was for only the limited purposes specifically enumerated in the Constitution. Within its limited sphere of power, the new national government was supreme, and any conflicting state laws had to give way – this is the message of the Supremacy Clause of Article VI. Beyond this limited sphere, however, the state governments continued to exist and exercise significant powers. In the words of James Madison in *Federalist No. 45*, "The powers delegated by the proposed Constitution to the federal government are few and defined. Those which are to remain in the State governments are numerous and indefinite. The former will be exercised principally on external objects, as war, peace, negotiation, and foreign commerce, with which last the power of taxation will, for the most part, be connected. The powers reserved to the several States will extend to all the objects which, in the ordinary course of affairs, concern the lives, liberties, and properties of the people, and the internal order, improvement, and prosperity of the State."

With this basic framework in place, the U.S. Constitution created a unique "federalist" structure of government, dividing sovereignty vertically between the federal and state governments. Contrary to the assertion of some on the political left, *federalism* isn't a dirty word. In fact, it's a concept critical for protecting individual liberty. The Supreme Court put it this way, in *New York v. United States* (1992): "The Constitution does not protect the sovereignty of States for the benefit of the States or state governments as abstract political entities, or even for the benefit of the public officials governing the States. To the contrary, the Constitution divides authority between federal and state governments for the protection of individuals. State sovereignty is not just an end in itself: 'Rather, federalism secures to citizens the liberties that derive from the diffusion of power.'" The Court reiterated this function of federalism in its unanimous decision in the 2011 case *Bond v. United States*: "By denying any one government complete jurisdiction over all the concerns of public life, federalism protects the liberty of the individual from arbitrary power. When government acts in excess of its lawful powers, that liberty is at stake." The Court's understanding of the purpose of federalism echoes that of *Federalist No. 51*, in which Madison described federalism as a "double security . . . to the rights of the people" because the federal and state governments "will control each other, at the same time that each will be controlled by itself."

The Constitution also divides government power horizontally, by segregating the national government into three distinct branches. Article I creates Congress and defines its limited powers, Article II creates the presidency and defines its limited powers, and Article III creates a federal judiciary and defines its limited powers.

Because Congress is the only branch of government constitutionally authorized to make laws, Article I is quite detailed in the kinds of laws that Congress is empowered to enact. Specifically, Article I, section 8, of the Constitution enumerates eighteen clauses, or power sources, on which federal laws may be based. If Congress wants to pass a law, the law must be grounded in one of those eighteen power sources; if not, the law is unconstitutional.

Tea Partiers ardently believe that these eighteen power sources should be taken seriously, not just given lip service or disregarded when inconvenient or inexpedient. If Congress doesn't have the power to pass a law – no matter how important or well intentioned the law may be – the law should be ruled unconstitutional by the judiciary. Principles, not politics, are what matter to the Tea Party.

Defending the principle of limited government depends on a sustained effort by all three branches of government. And although the judicial branch has been recognized as the final enforcer of the constitutional limits on federal power since the Supreme Court's 1803 decision in *Marbury v. Madison*, it is certainly not the first or only enforcer of these constitutional limits. As a matter of common sense, a principle so important cannot be solely entrusted to a single branch of government. What if, over time, the federal judiciary falls asleep at the wheel? What would happen if the Supreme Court succumbs to the temptation to look the other way as the executive and legislative branches push the envelope of their enumerated powers?

This was a possibility understood and feared by the founders. For example, in a letter to Charles Hammond in 1821, Thomas Jefferson confessed feeling anxiety about the judiciary's early willingness, under the leadership of ardent Federalist and Supreme Court Chief Justice John Marshall, to imply powers beyond those enumerated in the constitutional text:

> It has long, however, been my opinion, and I have never shrunk from its expression... that the germ of dissolution of our federal government is in the constitution of the federal judiciary; an irresponsible body (for impeachment is scarcely a scarecrow) working like gravity by night and by day, gaining a little today and little tomorrow, and advancing its noiseless step like a thief, over the field of jurisdiction, until all shall be usurped from the States, and the government of all be consolidated into one. To this I am opposed; because, when all government, domestic and foreign, in little as in great things, shall be drawn to Washington as the center of all power, it will render powerless the checks provided of one government or another, and will become as venal and oppressive as the government from which we separated.

Almost two hundred years after Jefferson's observation, ask yourself whether his anxiety was well founded. Has government power steadily marched away from the states and toward Washington, D.C.? Do the powers of the federal government seem to be ever expanding? If your answer to both those questions is yes, then you can reasonably reach one of two conclusions: (1) the Constitution's scheme of limited and enumerated powers is being disregarded and something needs to be done to change it; or (2) the Constitution may or may not have been disregarded, but it doesn't really matter because the concept of limited and enumerated powers isn't really all that relevant anymore. Tea Partiers fall in the first camp.

Tea Partiers believe that the Constitution is as binding today as it was in 1789, and the only legitimate way to change it is to pass a constitutional amendment. Under Article V, the Constitution can be amended after two-thirds of both houses of Congress (or a constitutional convention convened by two-thirds of the states) propose an amendment, which is subsequently ratified by three-quarters of state legislatures or state conventions. Although this is a high hurdle to overcome, it was made high on purpose by the founders, who believed that the blueprint of government they gave us was entitled to a presumption of legitimacy unless and until supermajorities of a future generation decided otherwise. Tea Partiers embrace this presumption of legitimacy of the U.S. Constitution and insist that the federal government remain a government of limited and enumerated powers only, until amended by the processes of Article V.

So how does the Tea Party's insistence on the enforcement of the principle of limited and enumerated powers translate into its positions on current issues? One area in which the translation is evident is Tea Partiers' criticism of runaway bailouts, bulging deficits, and the Federal Reserve. The Contract from America, for example, instructs Tea Party members to work to enact a constitutional amendment requiring "a balanced budget with a two-thirds majority needed for any tax hike." When it comes to the bailouts, Tea Partiers believe that nothing was really bailed out and, in fact, they made a bad economic situation even worse. A January 2011 Rasmussen

poll revealed that a majority of Americans (53 percent) believe
that in retrospect, spending trillions of dollars to bailout banks,
auto makers, insurers, and brokerage houses has been "bad
for the United States." Among Tea Partiers, the impression
is even direr: an April 2010 Winston Group poll found that 87
percent don't think the stimulus has worked at all.

When it comes to the Federal Reserve – the central bank
of the United States – the Tea Party's objections have an
intellectually deeper and richer history than most people realize. Tea Party concerns about both the constitutionality and
the pragmatic benefit of a central bank recently caused the
Republican Party of Maine to call for abolishing the Fed altogether. Similarly, Tea Party candidate Rand Paul, now U.S.
senator from Kentucky, declared on his Web site: "Excessive
spending, borrowing, and printing money are agents of debt
that are bankrupting this nation and drowning our Dollar.
The Federal Government is running back-breaking budget
deficits, amassing crippling debt, and borrowing trillions of
dollars from the Chinese to finance its extravagance. Mean-
while, the Federal Reserve, an unelected group of private
bankers, is printing trillions of dollars to bail out private industry, purchase government debt, and flood the market with
cheap credit." Rand Paul's objection seems related principally to the political unaccountability of the Federal Reserve,
an institution that isn't mentioned anywhere in the Constitution. Senator Paul's father, former presidential candidate and
congressman Ron Paul, has been even more explicit in his criticism, asserting in a speech on the floor of the House of Representatives that the Federal Reserve is blatantly unconstitutional: "Abolishing the Federal Reserve will allow Congress to
reassert its constitutional authority over monetary policy. The
United States Constitution grants to Congress the authority

to coin money and regulate the value of the currency. The Constitution does not give Congress the authority to delegate control over monetary policy to a central bank."

Opposition to the Federal Reserve is generally characterized in the media as fringe, semi-loony behavior. Yet there's been a long-standing and serious claim that a central bank is unconstitutional. Founding luminaries no less than Thomas Jefferson, James Madison, and the first attorney general, Edmund Randolph, all adamantly opposed the creation of a national bank, asserting that Congress lacked the power to create one. They argued that, of the eighteen power sources listed in Article I, section 8, none of them mention, or could be fairly interpreted to include, the power to create a national bank.

Secretary of the Treasury Alexander Hamilton, a strong Federalist, disagreed with Madison, Jefferson, and Randolph. Hamilton believed the power to create a national bank could be reasonably inferred by combining several enumerated powers, such as the power to coin money, to regulate commerce, and to tax and spend for the general welfare.

President George Washington was ultimately persuaded by Hamilton (they were both Federalists), and he signed the bill creating the first national bank into law. Decades later, in 1819, a Federalist-dominated Supreme Court, led by Chief Justice John Marshall, ruled that the central bank was constitutional. We'll talk more about the Court's decision in *McCulloch v. Maryland* when we analyze the constitutionality of Obamacare, but for now it suffices to say that, in this early debate about how broadly or narrowly to construe enumerated federal powers, the Supreme Court exhibited an eagerness to construe them quite broadly, thus confirming Jefferson's fears about the gradual, "noiseless" threat to limited powers posed by the judiciary.

Even after the Supreme Court's decision in *McCulloch*, in the 1830s President Andrew Jackson vetoed subsequent congressional reauthorization of the national bank, honoring his campaign promise to stop what he believed was an unconstitutional exercise of congressional power. The United States was without a central bank until 1913, when the Glass-Owen Act created the Federal Reserve, the current iteration of a national bank.

As the long battle over the constitutional legitimacy of a national bank shows, a debate about how much latitude is best in interpreting the eighteen enumerated congressional power sources has been raging since the country's founding. So when Tea Partiers carry signs saying "Stop Treading on the Constitution," "This Is Not What Our Ancestors Died For," and "Bigger Government = Less Freedom," they are continuing a cry begun by James Madison, Thomas Jefferson, and Edmund Randolph. It's a cry that exclaims the need to narrowly, not broadly, construe federal powers to preserve the principle of limited government. This principle isn't a fringe, modern, or right-wing concept; it's a uniquely American concept.

The modern battleground for defending the principle of limited and enumerated powers is health-care reform. The reform law, which has been dubbed "Obamacare," transfers massive new power to the federal government. If the Supreme Court ultimately upholds the constitutionality of Obamacare, there's arguably nothing off limits to Congress – other than perhaps the specific provisions of the Bill of Rights – turning the concept of limited government on its head. Health-care reform is the last stand.

Poll after poll shows that the majority of Americans oppose the health-reform law. Shortly after passage in March 2010, a Rasmussen poll showed that 55 percent of Americans favored repealing the law. By late July 2011, that number remained unchanged. Indeed, the same Rasmussen poll has indicated unwavering majority support for repeal every week since Obamacare's enactment, ranging from 50 percent to 63 percent. As of late July 2011, only 35 percent of Rasmussen respondents believed that Obamacare was "good for the country." Tea Partiers' opinion was even less favorable, with an April 2010 Gallup poll indicating that only 12 percent believed health reform was a "good thing" and an astonishing 87 percent believed it was a "bad thing."

U.S. Senator Scott Brown was the first to ride the wave of anger about Obamacare to electoral victory, capturing not only the Senate seat formerly occupied by liberal lion Ted Kennedy but also the attention of the nation, declaring in his victory speech: "One thing is clear, voters do not want the trillion-dollar health care bill that is being forced on the American people. This bill is not being debated openly and fairly. It will raise taxes, hurt Medicare, destroy jobs, and run our nation deeper into debt. It is not in the interest of our state or country – we can do better." When Congress ignored this sentiment and passed the bill a few weeks later, Americans' growing anger over runaway government gained a useful focal point. By the midterm elections of November 2010, anger over Obamacare propelled the Republicans – with the aid of the Tea Party movement – to retake the House of Representatives and gain six seats in the Senate.

Supporters of Obamacare have insinuated that opposition to the new law is somehow motivated by racism. This is illustrated by the constant, odd analogy drawn between health reform and civil rights reform. In a *New York Times* op-ed, for example, columnist Frank Rich opined, "To find a prototype for the overheated reaction to the health care bill, you have to look a year before Medicare, to the Civil Rights Act of 1964. Both laws passed by similar majorities in Congress.... But it was only the civil rights bill that made some Americans run off the rails. That's because it was the one that signaled an inexorable and immutable change in the very identity of America, not just its governance." Similarly, Democrat Senate Majority Leader Harry Reid said that Obamacare opponents were little different from those who opposed rights for blacks and women: "At pivotal points in American history, tactics of distortion and delay have ... been used to stop progress. That's what we're talking about here [with health reform]." Reid made the connection even clearer when he stated: "You think you've heard these same excuses before, you're right. When this country belatedly recognized the wrongs of slavery, there were those who dug in their heels and said, 'Slow down, it's too early. Let's wait. Things aren't bad enough.'" Even the president and his staff have compared the two. President Obama has dismissed the seriousness of legal challenges to health reform, saying, "When the Civil Rights Act was passed and the Voting Rights Act was passed, there were all kinds of lawsuits." His assistant for special projects, Stephanie Cutter, similarly stated on the official White House blog, "We saw this with the Social Security Act, the Civil Rights Act, and the Voting Rights Act – constitutional challenges were brought to all three of these monumental pieces of legislation, and all of those challenges failed."

These aren't random coincidences. There seems to be a concerted effort to link opposition to civil rights and opposition to Obamacare. Although they never come out and say it, the implication is clear: anger over Obamacare is little more than thinly veiled racism. This is becoming an all-too-common, knee-jerk response to any disagreement with President Obama's policies. Don't like Obamacare? Racism. Disagree with bailouts and mortgage relief? Racism. Oppose the president's stance on immigration or the war on terror? Racism. Frankly, it's getting old, like the boy who cried wolf.

The truth is that the Tea Partiers' steadfast opposition to Obamacare is based on a simple belief: it violates the constitutional principle of limited government. Adding pragmatic insult to constitutional injury, it "reforms" something that doesn't appear to most Americans to be broken, or at least not so broken that fixing it requires fundamentally transforming 17 percent of the national economy, vastly expanding federal power, invading the sovereignty of the states, and violating individual liberty.

The rarely admitted truth is that the American health-care system does an admirable job of providing prompt access to high-quality health care for the vast majority of people. A November 2010 Gallup poll – taken almost eight months after enactment of Obamacare – showed that 88 percent of Americans with private health insurance say that the quality of care they receive is either excellent (40 percent) or good (48 percent). Even among Americans without any health insurance, 53 percent rate their care as excellent (14 percent) or good (39 percent).

In addition to private insurance, several government-sponsored programs provide access to groups that are likely to have difficulty affording private health insurance, either because they're too poor or because they have chronic health conditions. Older Americans have Medicare. The poor have Medicaid. Veterans have the Veterans Administration health system. There are many county and rural health clinics scattered across the country.

Perhaps even more significant, every person in this country – citizen and noncitizen – has guaranteed access to emergency care, regardless of ability to pay, under a federal law called the Emergency Medical Treatment and Labor Act. Anyone who arrives at a hospital emergency room in an emergency condition is entitled to receive on-the-spot treatment. Although EMTALA doesn't require that hospitals provide their services for free – nor should it, anymore than grocers should be required to provide free food – the point is that access to emergency care is completely unfettered.

Of the Americans who remain uninsured, many are uninsured by choice, which means that they could qualify for private insurance but simply choose not to buy it. Thirty-eight percent of the uninsured make more than $50,000 per year; 39 percent are younger than age twenty-five; and 25 percent of them aren't U.S. citizens. Of the 39 percent who are younger than age twenty-five, most are predictably healthy and relatively inexpensive to insure. These demographic characteristics of the uninsured – young, healthy, working people – are what drive the individual mandate. Because Obamacare makes health insurance substantially more expensive – by prohibiting insurers from doing things like excluding those with preexisting conditions or charging substantially higher premiums for sick people – the Obama administration has confessed, in the words of Judge Hudson from the Eastern District of Virginia lawsuit, that "these features... will have a material effect on the health insurance underwriting process, and inevitably, the cost of insurance coverage. Therefore, without full market participation [i.e., the individual mandate], the financial foundation supporting the health care system will fail, in effect causing the entire health care regime to 'implode.' Unless everyone is required by law to purchase health insurance, or pay a penalty, the revenue base will be insufficient to underwrite the costs of insuring individuals presently considered as high risk or uninsurable."

Inherent in the individual mandate is a disturbing rationale: we need to mandate that these relatively young, healthy people buy a private product, health insurance, so that we can spread around their premium dollars, subsidizing the cost of insurance to older and sicker individuals. Also inherent is an acknowledgment that many of the uninsured are making an economically rational decision to forgo insurance, opting to spend their money on items they personally deem more valuable than health insurance, such as food, housing, clothing, cars, education, or electronics.

The individual mandate reflects a moral condemnation of an individual's choice to value, say, education over health insurance. The mandate demands that health insurance become the number-one spending priority of every uninsured American and penalizes those who spend their money elsewhere. Such nanny-state control over individual spending decisions regarding private goods and services is unprecedented. Whether it's lollipops, broccoli, cell phones, life insurance, or health insurance, the federal government has never before attempted to interfere with an individual's liberty to decide what private products to buy or forgo.

Americans' anger about the scope and impact of Obamacare is fueled by a commonsense awareness of its negative implications for individual liberty. This helps explain why, despite the Obama administration's initial belief that Americans would come to love the law with time, opposition hasn't subsided. Instead, lawsuits challenging Obamacare's constitutionality were filed by several states just moments after it was signed into law, represented by some of the best constitutional lawyers in the country, who've agreed to work for virtually nothing. The largest and most important of these lawsuits, initiated in Florida, now includes a mind-boggling lineup of twenty-six states.

Supporters of the health-reform law were quick to declare the lawsuits frivolous. A *Slate* magazine op-ed by Simon Lazarus and Alan Morrison, for example, accused the states challenging Obamacare of "grandstanding" and "flout[ing] in particular the federal procedural rules forbidding cases from being filed for 'an improper purpose.'" They concluded that the lawsuits were "legally frivolous" for "procedural reasons obvious to a first-year law student." That's a pretty serious accusation against more than half the states and their able lawyers. But lest you think Lazarus and Morrison are outliers or overly zealous ideologues, consider more recent op-eds written by liberal constitutional law luminaries Laurence Tribe and Erwin Chemerinsky. Writing in the *New York Times* in February 2011, Professor Tribe asserted that the lawsuits were just "a political objection in legal garb" because there's a "clear case for the law's constitutionality." Dean Chemerinsky was even more strident, writing in *Politico* that the lawsuits have "no basis in the law" and "no legal merit," and concluding that there's "no doubt" Obamacare is constitutional because, although "there is much to argue about in the debate over health care reform . . . constitutionality is not among the hard questions to consider."

Are these lawsuits really nothing more than political grandstanding? Is there any merit to the constitutional objections they raise? To answer these questions, we need to understand what the lawsuits are claiming and what the current state of the law is on those legal claims. Broken down to their core, the lawsuits challenging Obamacare rest on three primary constitutional arguments: (1) the individual mandate isn't supported by congressional power to regulate interstate commerce; (2) the individual mandate isn't supported by congressional taxing power; and (3) the law's expansion of Medicaid violates the principle of federalism embodied in provisions such as the Tenth Amendment. A few of the less prominent lawsuits also raise some claims relating to individual liberty and privacy.

Before getting into the details of these three constitutional arguments, let's address a commonly raised question: Aren't we required to buy insurance all the time? We have to buy car insurance if we want to drive a car. We sometimes have to buy homeowners' or flood insurance to get a mortgage. So if all these types of mandatory insurance are permissible, why isn't Obamacare's mandate to buy health insurance?

First, notice that only one of these mandatory insurance examples involves a governmentally imposed mandate – automobile insurance. Purchasing homeowners' or flood insurance isn't something the government is making you do. It's a contractual requirement imposed by your mortgage company. Private companies are free to establish the terms on which they'll do business with you. And of course you're free to decide whether you want to do business with them on the terms they offer. You don't have to have a mortgage, even assuming you'd rather own than rent. You have plenty of choices, and there's no government limiting those choices. Because there's no exercise of government power in these types of mandatory insurance, there's no constitutional issue involved.

When it comes to automobile insurance, however, the source of the mandate is indeed the government, not a private company. But is mandatory car insurance really analogous to mandatory health insurance under Obamacare? No, for this simple reason: the sovereign mandating car insurance is the state, not federal, government. And as discussed at the beginning of this chapter, the principle of limited government is a principle that applies to the federal government, not the states. As Madison explained in *Federalist No. 45*, "The powers delegated by the proposed Constitution to the federal government are few and defined. Those which are to remain in the State governments are numerous and indefinite." The "numerous and indefinite" powers remaining in state governments include what's commonly referred to as the police power, which, again in the words of *Federalist No. 45*, "extend[s] to all the objects which, in the ordinary course of affairs, concern the lives, liberties, and properties of the people, and the internal order, improvement, and prosperity of the State."

The police power is the most comprehensive power given to any government, allowing the government holding it to police, or protect, the life, liberty, and property of those in its borders. The police power gives rise to all criminal, tort, contract, and property law – all of which continue to belong almost exclusively to state governments. The founders consciously and explicitly rejected the idea of giving the federal government a police power. The federal government does have some power to protect its citizens, but only through the exercise of specific, constitutionally enumerated powers, not through a general police power.

State laws mandating the purchase of car insurance are the states' way of declaring that, to protect the lives and property of their people, having car insurance is a necessary prerequisite to being granted the privilege of obtaining a license to drive on the state's roads. By contrast, when a federal law like Obamacare mandates that citizens buy health insurance, there's no similar police power justification. The federal government simply doesn't have a police power. This also explains why states like Massachusetts can impose an individual mandate to buy health insurance without raising constitutional concerns. Massachusetts has a police power; the federal government doesn't.

It's critically important that Americans get this distinction: the federal government doesn't have the power to do anything it wants to do. It's a government of limited and enumerated powers only, so the $6 million constitutional question is this: which of the enumerated powers could conceivably permit the federal government to mandate that citizens buy health insurance?

The first and most important enumerated power source used to justify the health-reform law is the commerce power, which refers to language in Article I, section 8, giving Congress power to "regulate commerce with foreign nations, and among the several States, and with the Indian tribes." Specifically, the Obama administration claims that mandating the purchase of health insurance is a regulation of interstate ("among the several States") commerce, either because (1) failing to buy insurance is a commercial or economic activity by itself or (2) failing to buy insurance is something that, though not itself commercial or economic activity, has a substantial effect on commerce – namely, the national health insurance market. Because a mandate to buy health insurance is a useful means to effectuate Obamacare's broader health insurance market reforms, the commerce power, combined with the Necessary and Proper Clause of the Constitution, amply support the constitutionality of the individual mandate.

Before diving into Supreme Court cases interpreting the Commerce Clause, I should reveal a straw man that is regularly and misleadingly bandied about. Supporters of health reform, including the Obama administration itself, have from time to time pointed out that there's nothing unusual about a federal law that penalizes someone for a failure to do something. True enough. Citizens who don't pay their taxes or pay their taxes late are penalized for such failures to act. Similarly, citizens who don't register for the Selective Service or report for military duty can be punished.

But these are completely irrelevant to any principled assessment of the constitutionality of the health-reform law. Under a government of limited and enumerated powers, the first question one must ask is, What's the constitutional power source supporting the exercise of power? In the case of the individual mandate, the power sources relied on are (1) the Commerce Clause (either alone or augmented by the Necessary and Proper Clause) and (2) the taxing power. If neither one of these power sources will support the individual mandate, assessing a penalty for failing to buy health insurance is obviously also unconstitutional. You can't impose a penalty for failing to abide by a law that is unconstitutional.

In the example of failing to pay taxes (or failing to pay them on time), the penalties are constitutional because the underlying law itself – the tax code – is constitutional, grounded in the enumerated power of Congress "to lay and collect taxes." Similarly, punishing those who fail to register for Selective Service or report for military duty is constitutional because the law itself is grounded in Congress's enumerated powers to "raise and support armies," to "provide and maintain a navy," and to "make rules for the government and regulation of the land and naval forces." When it comes to Obamacare, therefore, the salient question is whether the individual mandate itself is constitutional. If it's not, the penalty can't be enforced. And because the enumerated powers relied on to support Obamacare are the commerce and taxing powers, we are right back where we started, trying to ascertain whether the individual mandate is a constitutional exercise of the commerce or taxing powers.

A. THE COMMERCE POWER

Litigation over health reform focuses on four big Supreme Court decisions interpreting the reach of the Commerce Clause. These four cases can be conceptualized as dueling pairs. On the one hand, there's a pair of cases representing the high-water mark of the commerce power: *Wickard v. Filburn* (1942) and *Gonzales v. Raich* (2005). On the other hand, there's a pair of cases representing the only successful attempts in more than seventy years to limit the commerce power: *United States v. Lopez* (1995) and *United States v. Morrison* (2000).

Let's examine first the two principal cases relied on by the Obama Administration: *Wickard v. Filburn* and *Gonzales v. Raich*. In *Wickard*, the plaintiff was a farmer who violated a New Deal law called the Agricultural Adjustment Act, by growing twelve acres more wheat than the quota allotted to him by the act. The farmer demonstrated that he used the excess wheat solely for home consumption, making bread, feeding his livestock, and so on. None of the excess was sold or otherwise entered the stream of interstate commerce.

He argued that, because this homegrown wheat was neither "interstate" nor "commercial" in nature, it was beyond the reach of the Commerce Clause.

The Supreme Court in *Wickard* disagreed with the farmer, ruling that his homegrown wheat was within the reach of the commerce power. The Court reasoned that by growing excess wheat, the farmer was affecting the interstate market for wheat because, without such homegrown wheat, the farmer would have to buy it in the open market. The Court declared, "That [Farmer Filburn's] own contribution to the demand for wheat may be trivial by itself is not enough to remove him from the scope of federal regulation where, as here, his contribution, taken together with that of many others similarly situated, is far from trivial." In other words, because Farmer Filburn's activity of growing extra wheat was substantial when combined with all other farmers doing the same thing, his intrastate, noncommercial activity could be regulated by the interstate commerce clause. This became known as the aggregation principle.

The aggregation principle was also the basis of the Supreme Court's 2005 decision in *Gonzales v. Raich*, the other big case relied on by Obamacare supporters. *Raich* involved a challenge to the federal Controlled Substances Act (CSA), which prohibits any sale, possession, or use of marijuana. The plaintiffs in *Raich* used marijuana to treat their serious illnesses, pursuant to a "compassionate use" law in California that allowed doctors to prescribe marijuana for medicinal purposes. Even though California's law allowed the plaintiffs' use of marijuana, the federal CSA didn't, and under the Constitution's Supremacy Clause, a valid federal law trumps conflicting state law. So the question in *Raich* was: is the CSA, as applied to individuals using medicinal marijuana allowed by state law, constitutional?

Because the constitutional power source for the CSA was the Commerce Clause, the act's constitutionality turned on whether the Commerce Clause could properly reach the intrastate, noncommercial growth, possession, and consumption of marijuana. As you can see from this brief description, the facts of *Raich* were remarkably similar to those in *Wickard*. In both cases, a citizen claimed he was engaging in an activity – growing and consuming wheat or growing and consuming pot – that was solely intrastate, and noncommercial in character, and outside the reach of the federal commerce power. It shouldn't be surprising, therefore, to find that the *Raich* Court ruled the exact same way as the *Wickard* Court. The *Raich* majority relied heavily on *Wickard*, declaring, "Our case law firmly establishes Congress'[s] power to regulate purely local activities that are part of an economic 'class of activities' that have a substantial effect on interstate commerce." Because growing pot at home for medicinal purposes could have a "substantial effect" on the illicit interstate market for recreational pot, the fact that the plaintiffs' pot was grown and consumed locally, and neither bought nor sold, didn't exempt it from the Commerce Clause.

Beyond *Wickard* and *Raich*, supporters of Obamacare also sometimes cite a pair of Commerce Clause cases from the 1960s involving the Civil Rights Act: *Heart of Atlanta Motel v. United States* and *Katzenbach v. McClung*. Both *Heart of Atlanta* and *Katzenbach* involved constitutional challenges to section 201 of the Civil Rights Act of 1964, which prohibited discrimination or segregation in "places of public accommodation" on the basis of race, color, religion, or national origin. The act defined places of public accommodation as follows: (1) lodging places such as hotels and motels; (2) facilities that sell food for on-site consumption, such as restaurants; (3) places of exhibition or entertainment, such as theaters, sports arenas, and concert halls; and (4) any establishment physically located within the premises of any of the three types of establishments.

Section 201 explicitly stated that the Civil Rights Act reached only those places of public accommodation "if its operations affect commerce." It then defined the meaning of "affect commerce," concluding that (1) lodging places per se affected commerce; (2) restaurants affected commerce if they "serve or offer to serve interstate travelers or a substantial portion of the food which it serves or gasoline or other products which it sells, has moved in commerce"; and (3) a place of exhibition or entertainment affected commerce if it "customarily presents films, performances, athletic teams, exhibitions, or other sources of entertainment which move in commerce." The critical thing to notice is that, for all types of public accommodation identified, the act demanded that the facility buy or rely on goods or services that moved across state lines. Why did the Civil Rights Act of 1964 contain such strange language? For the simple reason that by including a "movement in commerce" hook, the law could be justified as an exercise of the commerce power.

In both cases proprietors of businesses – a large motel located in downtown Atlanta in *Heart of Atlanta* and a small barbeque restaurant located in Birmingham, Alabama, in *Katzenbach* – argued that the act wasn't a valid exercise of the commerce power. They claimed their businesses were located in a single state and couldn't be considered as engaging in interstate commerce. The Supreme Court rejected this argument, concluding that the activity targeted by the Civil Rights

Act – discrimination by proprietors of public accommodations on the basis of race, color, religion, or national origin – had, in aggregate, a substantial effect on interstate commerce. The Court found that Congress had created an ample record establishing this negative effect on commerce, with extensive testimony showing that, for example, blacks who wanted to travel from Massachusetts to Florida were often deterred from doing so, for fear that they couldn't find appropriate places to stay and eat along their journey. The chilling effect of discrimination impeded the interstate movement of travelers and thus the free and robust flow of interstate commerce.

Supporters of the health-reform law have suggested that *Heart of Atlanta* and *Katzenbach* support the constitutionality of the individual mandate. They characterize both cases as involving a federal law – the Civil Rights Act of 1964 – that targeted "inactivity" – namely, the failure of hotels, restaurants, and other places of public accommodation to serve people on the basis of race, color, religion, or national origin. Dean Chemerinsky, for example, tried to make this argument in an October 2010 op-ed in *Politico*: "The court has said that Congress can use its commerce power to forbid hotels and restaurants from discriminating based on race, even though their conduct was refusing to engage in commercial activity." Similarly, Eastern District of Michigan federal trial judge George Steeh's early decision to dismiss a Commerce Clause challenge to Obamacare in *Thomas More Law Center v. Obama* made the same connection, asserting that *Heart of Atlanta* stands for the proposition that the "Commerce Clause allows Congress to regulate decisions not to engage in transactions with persons with whom plaintiff did not wish to deal."

But this is a gross mischaracterization of *Heart of Atlanta* and *Katzenbach*. The Civil Rights Act, by its explicit terms, didn't target "inactivity" – that is, the failure of businesses to serve blacks. Instead, the Civil Rights Act's language is very carefully chosen, targeting specific, affirmative acts of discrimination by businesses engaging in interstate commerce. Hotels, for example, are deemed to "affect commerce" because they serve, or offer to serve, interstate travelers. Restaurants "affect commerce" under the act if they buy food that has traveled in commerce or serve and/or offer to serve interstate customers. Sports arenas and movie theaters "affect commerce" if they show films or use actors or athletes who have traveled in commerce. These commercial establishments targeted by the Civil Rights Act operate within the stream of commerce 24/7.

The elaborate statutory language in the Civil Rights Act of 1964 is very different from Obamacare's individual mandate, which merely declares that "[a]n applicable individual shall for each month beginning after 2013 ensure that the individual, and any dependent of the individual who is an applicable individual, is covered under minimum essential coverage for each month." Notice that the individual mandate's language – unlike section 201 of the Civil Rights Act of 1964 – doesn't target any activity involving interstate commerce. All one can reasonably discern from the language of the individual mandate is that one has to be "an applicable individual" – that is, alive and not specifically excluded from the mandate.

A federal law that targets a failure to buy health insurance by anyone living isn't the same as a federal law that targets discrimination based on race, color, religion, or national origin while conducting business that "affects commerce" in well-defined ways. The former penalizes individual inactivity with no obvious connection to interstate commerce; the latter penalizes specific activity by businesses that affect interstate commerce in well-defined ways. Merely being alive isn't the same as engaging in constant commercial activity.

Now that we have a good sense of the case law relied on by Obamacare's supporters, let's analyze and compare the two principal cases relied on by the law's challengers: *United States v. Lopez* and *United States v. Morrison*. In *Lopez*, the Supreme Court struck down the federal Gun Free School Zones Act (GFSZA) as beyond the commerce power. The GFSZA made it a federal crime to carry a gun near a school zone. The government defended the law by arguing that guns near schools increased crime and distracted kids and teachers from learning. When all instances of carrying guns near schools were aggregated, argued the government, interstate commerce was negatively affected: students who can't learn, and teachers who can't teach, harm the economy by reducing productivity.

The Court rejected the government's broad view of the substantial-effects doctrine, observing that it required piling "inference upon inference in a manner that would bid fair to convert congressional authority under the Commerce Clause to a general police power of the sort retained by the States." It then confessed, "Admittedly, some of our prior cases [e.g., *Wickard*] have taken long steps down that road, giving great deference to congressional action. The broad language of these opinions has suggested the possibility of additional expansion, but we decline here to proceed any further."

The *Lopez* Court also concluded that the GFSZA was "a criminal statute that by its terms has nothing to do with 'commerce' or any sort of economic enterprise, however broadly one might define those terms." In other words, carrying a gun wasn't "economic activity." It was just an ordinary crime, devoid of the usual characteristics associated with economic activity. It didn't involve anything of value being bought, sold, or exchanged. Accordingly, the federal law was not a permissible exercise of congressional power to regulate interstate commerce.

The second case relied on by challengers of Obamacare is *United States v. Morrison* (2000), involving a Commerce Clause challenge to the federal Violence Against Women Act (VAWA). VAWA made it a federal crime to commit an act of violence against a woman, essentially duplicating state laws covering the same kinds of acts. The government defended VAWA in much the same way it did in *Lopez* – by arguing that women who were victims of violence were less likely to go to work, school, travel, shop, and so on, resulting in a productivity decline harmful to the national economy. The *Morrison* Court employed reasoning similar to *Lopez*, concluding that: (1) violent acts against women were not economic activities, but just ordinary crimes; and (2) such acts, in the aggregate, couldn't rationally be characterized as having a substantial effect on interstate commerce.

The bottom line in both *Lopez* and *Morrison* is that to be valid as an exercise of the commerce power, a federal law must either: (1) regulate economic activity or (2) regulate noneconomic activity that can rationally be said to have a substantial effect on interstate commerce. In either case, there has to be some underlying activity. Let's now proceed to examine whether Obamacare's individual mandate falls in either of these two categories.

1. *Economic Activity?*

Challengers of the health-reform law assert that not buying a private product (health insurance) can't be economic activity because it's neither economic nor activity. Because the substantial-effects argument also hinges on activity, I will put off a discussion of what *activity* means until we discuss the substantial-effects doctrine. For now, let's focus on the word *economic*.

Is failing to buy something economic in nature? Opponents of Obamacare answer no, for the commonsense reason that not buying something is inherently anticommercial, anti-economic. Like carrying a gun near a school (as in *Lopez*) or committing an act of violence against a woman (as in *Morrison*), failing to buy health insurance lacks a commercial or economic essence. Nothing is being bought or sold. Nothing of value is being exchanged. In fact, nothing is happening at all.

2. *Noneconomic Activity with a Substantial Effect on Commerce?*

The more challenging question for Obamacare, however, isn't whether failing to buy something is economic activity. It seems pretty obvious that it's not. The harder question is whether failing to buy something is noneconomic activity that has a substantial effect on interstate commerce – something the Supreme Court has endorsed in cases like *Wickard* and *Raich*.

But even this sweeping category has always required the identification of some activity being targeted for regulation, whether it be growing wheat as in *Wickard*, growing and using marijuana as in *Raich*, carrying a gun near a school as in *Lopez*, or committing an act of violence against a woman as in *Morrison*. In every one of these cases, the individual has committed some volitional act that triggers a claim (unsuccessful in *Lopez* and *Morrison*) that the act, when aggregated with other volitional acts of the same nature, has a substantial effect on interstate commerce.

The Obama administration argues that activity isn't required under the Commerce Clause. Instead, it claims that any economic decision that has a substantial effect on commerce is fair game. A person who doesn't buy health insurance, the argument goes, may not be undertaking an *activity* but is surely making a *decision* that, when aggregated with all such individuals making the same decision, substantially affects interstate commerce. When an uninsured person gets sick, the cost of his or her care is ultimately borne by hospitals, doctors, and other taxpayers. The economic decision to remain uninsured affects the broader interstate market for health care by raising and shifting costs.

Although the uninsured may seem to have opted out of the health insurance market altogether, in reality, the administration contends, no one can really opt out of this market. The uninsured have made a choice about the method of paying for their health care, analogous to paying by credit card rather than by check. And without insurance, the credit card debt they rack up – or at least a good deal of it – is paid by the rest of society.

The administration's shift from activity to decisions is novel. There's no Supreme Court precedent that has ever dared to go this far, endorsing the idea that merely *deciding* whether to do something should be the functional equivalent of actually doing something. The specter of thought police looms large.

Under the administration's theory, any decision we make becomes the functional equivalent of an activity that could, in the aggregate, have a substantial effect on interstate commerce. The decision whether to buy something always affects – by definition – the market for that product. As Judge Vinson said in favor of the states challenging health reform, "The decisions of whether and when (or not) to buy a house, a car, a television, a dinner, or even a morning cup of coffee also have a financial impact that – when aggregated with similar economic decisions – affect the price of that particular product or service and have a substantial effect on interstate commerce." He concluded, "To be sure, it is not difficult to identify an economic decision that has a cumulatively substantial effect on interstate commerce; rather, the difficult task is to find a decision that does not."

Although prior Supreme Court precedents have stretched the substantial-effects doctrine quite far, its use as a justification for Obamacare would be unprecedented. The federal government has never before asserted that the power to regulate interstate commerce includes the power to force citizens to buy a private product. Deciding what products to purchase is the essence of individual liberty, and a government that can interfere with this liberty is a Leviathan indeed.

Ordinary Americans are petrified about the scope of the power proposed by Obamacare. They're waiting for the left to articulate some limiting principle, some end point beyond which the Commerce Clause can't go, other than ordinary crimes like carrying a gun to school or committing an act of violence against a woman. The political left seems to be trying to identify such a limit. But their proposed limits are less than reassuring.

The first attempt at articulating a limiting principle for the Commerce Clause is that health care is "unique." The Obama administration claims, for example, that everyone will require health care at some point in their life. So sustaining a mandate to buy health insurance won't set a precedent allowing government to force people to buy other things like cars or shoes or broccoli. But what's so unique about health care? The Obama administration argues that it's unique because no one can opt out of the health-care market, and as a result, the costs of health care for the uninsured are often shifted onto hospitals, doctors, taxpayers, and those with health insurance.

But this isn't actually unique to health care at all. People can't really opt out of the food market, the water market, the clothing market, or even the housing market. Everyone has to have food, water, clothing, and some sort of housing. And once they enter these markets, if they fail to pay for the food, water, clothing, or housing they've received, the cost of the bad debt incurred by businesses that provided these goods will undoubtedly be passed along to other consumers in the form of higher costs.

Moreover, the premise on which the administration's uniqueness argument is made isn't even accurate. Some people can opt out of the health insurance market for their entire lives and never shift costs onto others. It's entirely conceivable that a person can be born, live a healthy life, and die peacefully at home without ever incurring a health care debt they can't pay. They might buy aspirin, over-the-counter cold remedies, go see a doctor, and even go to the hospital without shifting costs onto someone else. They may not have health insurance, but being uninsured doesn't automatically equate with being a deadbeat. Many people successfully self-insure for their health-care costs, setting aside sufficient personal savings to cover the costs of their own health care. Indeed, this is the basic premise behind medical savings accounts, which work well for many people. Others may incur health-care costs they're unable to pay immediately but work out a payment plan with the provider that pays their debt in full. Still others may receive help paying their bills from various charities, whose financial assistance could hardly be considered cost shifting that adversely affects the national economy. The bottom line, as Judge Vinson said in the Florida case, is, "Uniqueness is not an adequate limiting principle as every market problem is, at some level and in some respects, unique. If Congress asserts power that exceeds its enumerated powers, then it is unconstitutional, regardless of the purported uniqueness of the context in which it is being asserted."

The second limiting principle identified by the left is that to claim that forcing people to buy something is meaningfully different from forcing them to use or consume it. At a hearing of the Senate Judiciary Committee in February 2011, for example, Senator Dick Durbin asked Harvard law professor Charles Fried the following: "[P]eople are saying, '[W]ell, if the government can require me to buy health insurance, can it require me to have a membership in a gym, or eat vegetables?'.... [W]ould you like to comment?" Fried replied, "[T]hat would be a violation of the Fifth and the Fourteenth Amendment [Due Process Clauses] to force you to *eat* something. But to force you to *pay for* something, I don't see why not. It may not be a good idea, but I don't see why it's unconstitutional." Dean Chemerinsky likewise told Reason TV in August 2010 that "what people choose to *eat* well might be regarded as a personal liberty," but "Congress could use its commerce power to require people to *buy cars*."

Law professor Mark Hall articulated a similar limiting principle, "Comprehensive authority to regulate national markets still does not allow Congress to force people to *eat* broccoli, or to require people to post billboards on their houses, or to make storeowners open on Sunday mornings, or to mandate purchases only on one side of the Mississippi River or only in states that vote for Democrats. Each of these, and many other examples, would violate one of many other constitutional norms that continue to fence arbitrary or abusive federal power, even if purchase mandates are permitted."

As an initial matter, Professor Hall's reference to the Bill of Rights and other rights-protecting constitutional provisions isn't a limiting principle of the Commerce Clause. The Bill of Rights is a limiting principle on all exercises of government power. Hall is effectively saying, "Don't worry. Even if Congress can force you to buy stuff, the Bill of Rights is still in effect." But nobody seriously thinks that the Commerce Clause would override, for example, freedom of speech or religion under the First Amendment. So of course Congress couldn't force you to post a billboard on your house or open your business on Sunday morning. And Professor Hall's assurance that Congress can't "mandate purchases only on one side of the Mississippi River or only in states that vote for Democrats" is not very reassuring either. Such discriminatory actions against citizens who live on the "wrong side" of the Mississippi or in states that vote Republican would be irrational and hence violate the Equal Protection Clause.

Under the limiting principle articulated by Fried, Hall, and Chemerinsky, we're supposed to believe that Congress can force us to buy anything it wants us to buy – cars, shoes, broccoli, gym memberships, and other goods and services – yet Congress can't force us to use or consume those things. It can't make us drive the car, wear the shoes, eat the broccoli, or go to the gym. It can only make us buy them. This isn't much of a limiting principle.

Interestingly, Fried, Hall, and Chemerinsky all base their buying-versus-consuming distinction on the word *liberty* in the Due Process Clause. Yet there's no established constitutional liberty to eat what you want, drive what kind of car you want, or exercise if you want. We take freedom of choice in such matters for granted because no government – state or federal – has ever mounted a serious attempt to interfere with these freedoms.

But there have been laws enacted around the margins, chipping away at our freedom, for example, to make dietary choices. California, for example, has enacted a state law banning force-fed foie gras beginning in 2012. Chicago's City Council enacted a total foie gras ban in 2006, only to repeal it two years later. New York City, Philadelphia, and California have banned the use of trans fats in restaurants. The Scottish favorite, haggis, is banned nationwide because it contains sheep's lungs. And of course the federal Food and Drug Administration has broad authority – under a Commerce Clause-based law, no less – to ban foods it deems "adulterated" or "misbranded."

These laws restricting our food choices are admittedly limited, but who's to say with any confidence that government couldn't intrude further? Because there's no definitive case law protecting a liberty to eat what we want, a Commerce Clause-based federal law mandating that we eat our veggies could well be constitutional in the eyes of the legal scholars such as Fried, Chemerinsky, and Hall. After all, if eating our veggies would really make us all healthier, why not benevolently force us to do the right thing? Is there really any difference between forcing us to buy health insurance and forcing us to eat our veggies? Consider the rationale for upholding health reform offered by Professor Tribe in the

New York Times, "Those [trial court] judges [ruling Obamacare unconstitutional] made the confused assertion that what is at stake here is a matter of personal liberty – the right not to purchase what one wishes not to purchase – rather than the reach of national legislative power in a world where no man is an island."

Tribe's reasoning is frightening because it's realistic. He's telling us that there's no constitutional right to decide what to purchase. To him, the salient question is the "reach of legislative power in a world where no man is an island." If buying or not buying X affects interstate commerce – and why wouldn't it? – the legislature should be able to regulate your decision regarding whether to buy (or not buy) X. The same logic applies to your decision to eat, consume, or otherwise use X. All these decisions – buying/not buying, eating/not eating, using/not using – will affect commerce in a direct and substantial way. Because progressives think "no man is an island," every decision they make – including whether to eat their veggies – is within the reach of the Commerce Clause.

Boiled down to its essence, the fight about the substantial-effects doctrine of the Commerce Clause is whether the judiciary can be convinced that there's no real difference between activity and inactivity. In classic Orwellian doublethink – where black becomes white, in contradiction of obvious facts – the Obama administration would have us believe that inactivity is really just a form of activity, because there's really is no such thing, in today's interconnected world, as inactivity. Everything, in some way, has a substantial effect on the economy.

This logic should frighten ordinary Americans. If it's accepted by the courts, then the Commerce Clause becomes a police power, capable of reaching every decision we make.

There's no discernible limiting principle to this theory. And without a discernible limiting principle, there can be no principle of limited government.

3. *The Necessary and Proper Clause*

Even if the Supreme Court doesn't buy the doublethink notion that inactivity is activity, there's one final and critically important additional constitutional argument it must address: the Necessary and Proper Clause. At the very end of Article I, section 8, the Constitution gives Congress the power "[t]o make all laws which shall be necessary and proper for carrying into execution the foregoing powers." By its very terms, the Necessary and Proper Clause isn't a power source that can stand alone. In metaphorical terms, it's icing, not the cake itself. To enjoy the sweetness of the Necessary and Proper Clause, the government must first build a constitutionally permissible cake, based on one of the other enumerated powers.

The Obama administration contends that the individual mandate is constitutional because the law contains extensive reforms of the private health insurance market. And because the Supreme Court, since *United States v. South-Eastern Underwriters Association* (1944), has ruled that regulating insurance is a regulation of interstate commerce, the insurance market reforms provide the cake on which the individual mandate rests, employing the icing of the Necessary and Proper Clause.

This can get complicated, so let's be specific here. The argument goes like this: (1) Congress has authority under the Commerce Clause to regulate insurance, (2) the health reform law regulates health insurance extensively, and (3) the individual mandate is a necessary and proper way to effectuate the law's health insurance market reforms.

The best way to understand the reach of the Necessary and Proper Clause is to examine the seminal case interpreting it, *McCulloch v. Maryland* (1819). In *McCulloch*, the Supreme Court upheld the constitutionality of the Bank of the United States using the Necessary and Proper Clause, linking it to several other enumerated power sources in Article I, section 8. The *McCulloch* Court admitted that none of the enumerated powers in Article I, section 8, included the power to "create a bank" or "charter a corporation" such as a bank. But Chief Justice John Marshall's opinion said that the Necessary and Proper Clause could nonetheless help sustain the creation of a national bank, by giving Congress a choice of means to carry out the other enumerated powers. Interestingly, Marshall chose to broadly interpret the word *necessary*, concluding that it didn't mean "indispensible" or "absolutely necessary," but merely "convenient" or "useful."

With this definition in mind, *McCulloch* then concluded that a central bank was a convenient and useful way to carry out the enumerated powers to tax, spend, borrow money, declare war, raise and support an army and navy, and regulate commerce. Marshall reasoned:

> Throughout this vast republic, from the St. Croix to the Gulf of Mexico, from the Atlantic to the Pacific, revenue is to be collected and expended, armies are to be marched and supported. The exigencies of the nation may require, that the treasure raised in the north should be transported to the south, that raised in the east, conveyed to the west, or that this order should be reversed. Is that construction of the constitution to be preferred, which would render these operations difficult, hazardous and expensive? Can we adopt that construction

(unless the words imperiously require it), which would impute to the framers of that instrument, when granting these powers for the public good, the intention of imped-ing their exercise, by withholding a choice of means?

As you can see from *McCulloch*, the Necessary and Proper Clause is a useful adjunct to the enumerated powers. As inter-preted by the Supreme Court, it gives Congress broad discre-tion to figure out the best, most effective means for carrying out the enumerated powers. Although it's not a power source by itself, it instructs the judiciary to give Congress substantial wiggle room in deciding the best method by which to effec-tuate its enumerated powers. The most widely quoted test for whether the Necessary and Proper Clause constitution-ally supports a federal law was articulated by Chief Justice Marshall in *McCulloch*:

> We admit, as all must admit, that the powers of the government are limited, and that its limits are not to be transcended. But we think the sound construction of the constitution must allow to the national legislature that discretion with respect to the means by which the pow-ers it confers are to be carried into execution which will enable that body to perform the high duties assigned to it, in the manner most beneficial to the people. Let the end be legitimate, let it be within the scope of the con-stitution, and all means which are appropriate, which are plainly adapted to that end, which are not prohibited, but consistent with the letter and spirit of the constitution, are constitutional.

Marshall further clarified that if executing congressional power is a "pretext" for accomplishing objectives not within enumerated powers, court would have to declare it unconstitutional: "Should congress, in the execution of its powers, adopt measures which are prohibited by the constitution, or should congress, under the pretext of executing its powers, pass laws for the accomplishment of objects not intrusted to the government, it would become the painful duty of this tribunal, should a case requiring such a decision come before it, to say that such an act was not the law of the land."

To understand better how *McCulloch*'s test will affect the constitutional assessment of the individual mandate, let's carefully parse its elements:

1. The end must be legitimate.
2. The end must be within scope of the Constitution.
3. The means chosen by Congress must be plainly adapted to that legitimate end.
4. The means chosen by Congress must be consistent with letter and spirit of the Constitution.

If all four of these elements are satisfied, the federal law in question is constitutional, grounded in an enumerated power source, augmented by the Necessary and Proper Clause.

In the case of Obamacare, the "legitimate end" identified is the regulation of commerce – specifically, the regulation of the national health insurance market. These regulations include such things as forbidding insurers from excluding those with preexisting health conditions, eliminating lifetime caps on benefits, limiting premium variations, and mandating coverage of minors on parents' policies up to age twenty-six. Under the second prong of the *McCulloch* test, this "legitimate end" must be "within the scope of the constitution." This is essentially redundant, because by definition a "legitimate" end is "within the scope of the constitution." Because the Supreme Court has concluded that insurance is a form of commerce, the health-reform law's regulation of the national health insurance market satisfies both prongs one and two of *McCulloch*.

The third prong of *McCulloch* gets tricky. Is the individual mandate a "mean" that is "plainly adapted" to achieve the legitimate end of regulating the health insurance market? The difficulty is that an individual mandate isn't a method or mean of regulating insurance. It's a regulation of individual conduct. The individual mandate doesn't regulate health insurance in the same way, for example, as a ban on excluding preexisting conditions or eliminating lifetime coverage caps does. All the other market reforms of Obamacare are clearly market reforms – that is, they address the manner or means by which insurance is designed or sold.

The individual mandate, by contrast, is a regulation aimed at ordinary people, not insurance. It says to citizens, "Thou shalt buy insurance." Such a command may indeed help the insurance market, especially because Obamacare's market reforms have made health insurance a very expensive and risky thing to underwrite. But the individual mandate, by itself, isn't a means of achieving the legitimate end of regulating insurance as insurance.

When considering *McCulloch*'s fourth prong – that the law be "consistent with the letter and spirit of the constitution" – the negative impression about the individual mandate is reinforced. The founders never dreamed the commerce power would be interpreted so broadly as to give Congress the power to force citizens to buy private products. Forcing individuals to buy private goods or services, in the name of "regulating" interstate commerce, is contrary to the "letter and spirit of the constitution." Indeed, using the Necessary and Proper Clause to sustain the individual mandate seems to fall squarely within *McCulloch*'s warning about Congress, "under the pretext of executing its powers" passing laws "for the accomplishment of objects not intrusted to the government." The Obama administration is trying to convince the courts that, as a consequence of radically reforming the health insurance market, it needs the individual mandate to make these reforms work. Obamacare's market reforms, in other words, created a "crisis" in the health insurance market that can be avoided only by implementation of the individual mandate.

Obamacare's health insurance market reforms have rendered the health insurance market unstable, making it difficult for insurers to accurately estimate risk and consequently causing the cost of health insurance to spiral upward. The individual mandate is asserted to be "necessary" to offset these market reforms, because it helps sustain the viability of the health insurance market itself. Under the guise of executing the power to regulate the health insurance market (commerce), the health-reform law imposed an individual mandate, thereby accomplishing an object not otherwise entrusted to Congress (the power to force individuals to buy a private product). This is precisely the pretext situation Chief Justice Marshall was referring to in *McCulloch*.

Moreover, as Marshall prefaced his disquisition on the reach of the Necessary and Proper Clause, "We admit, as all must admit, that the powers of the government are limited, and that its limits are not to be transcended." If the Necessary and Proper Clause, annexed to the Commerce Clause, gives the federal government the power to force us to buy whatever it deems useful or convenient for bolstering any segment of the American economy, there's no limited government anymore.

B. THE TAXING POWER

After the Commerce Clause, the second argument made in most of the lawsuits challenging Obamacare relates to Congress's power to tax and spend for the general welfare. Contrary to the understanding of many, Congress does not have a power to pass laws for the general welfare simpliciter. It has a power to tax – and by necessary implication, spend tax dollars raised for the general welfare. In the context of Obamacare, the administration argues that the individual mandate, if invalid under the Commerce Clause, is nonetheless constitutional because it's based on Congress's power to tax. It asserts that those who don't buy health insurance will simply pay a tax for noncompliance with the individual mandate.

Before delving into the finer details about what makes a tax a tax, it's important to realize that there's a major constitutional difference between a law grounded on Congress's power to regulate commerce and one grounded on Congress's power to tax. Medicare, Medicaid, and Social Security, for example, are all exercises of congressional taxing power. They're funded by dedicated and general tax revenues, and these revenues are spent to carry out these programs.

If Obamacare had simply expanded Medicare or Medicaid, making them available to all uninsured, there would be no constitutional problem. Medicare and Medicaid are supported by the taxing power and expanding these programs wouldn't alter their constitutionality. And as we'll discover in a minute, there are specific things courts look for when determining whether Congress has exercised its taxing power. But none of these indicia are present with health reform's individual mandate. So although there were perfectly constitutional ways Congress could have provided universal health coverage – including using its taxing power – these ways weren't chosen in Obamacare. Instead, Obamacare opted to expand access using an unprecedented individual mandate, and it's this mandate that's being constitutionally challenged.

Much confusion about Obamacare is caused by conflating the power to regulate commerce and the power to tax. But these two power sources are unique, with their own sets of rules and court precedents to consult. Even Professor Tribe seemed to confuse the two power sources in his February 2011 op-ed in the *New York Times*, declaring "the health care law is little different from Social Security." Tribe made this statement in the context of pointing out that people can't opt out of Social Security because it would undermine the financial stability of the program. He was trying to analogize Social Security to Obamacare, arguing that Obamacare also couldn't let people opt out of buying health insurance because, in light of the laws' new insurance market reforms, allowing people to opt out would undermine the financial stability of the health insurance market itself.

But Tribe knows better – Social Security doesn't have to provide an opt out because it's an exercise of the taxing and spending power. If Congress wants to raise taxes to fund a Social Security program, it has virtually unlimited discretion to determine who, exactly, pays Social Security taxes and how much they pay. Obamacare, by contrast, isn't an exercise of the taxing power, for reasons that will be clear in a moment. Instead, Obamacare is supposedly grounded in the commerce power. And if the Commerce Clause doesn't authorize forcing citizens to buy health insurance, it can't by definition have the same sort of mandatory opt in that Social Security has. The taxing and spending power and the commerce power are apples and oranges – what's allowed under one power source isn't necessarily allowed under another.

So why can't the individual mandate of Obamacare be grounded in the taxing and spending power? The short answer is because the individual mandate imposes a penalty, not a tax, on those who fail to buy health insurance. The Supreme Court has said that, when figuring out whether something is a tax or a penalty, the overriding consideration is congressional intent. Did Congress intend to exercise its taxing authority?

In ascertaining congressional intent, courts first look to the language of the specific statutory provision in question. The individual mandate of Obamacare – Section 1501 – says, "If an applicable individual fails to meet the requirement of subsection (a) [by purchasing health insurance] . . . there is hereby imposed a penalty." So the individual mandate's plain language purports to impose a penalty rather than a tax.

The next thing courts consider is the language elsewhere in the statute. What constitutional power source, if any, did Congress indicate it was attempting to exercise? Are there other places in the statute that use the word *tax*? The answer to both these questions suggests that Congress didn't intend noncompliance with the individual mandate to result in a tax. Section 1501 contains findings of fact that declare, for example, that "[t]he individual . . . [mandate] is commercial and economic in nature, and substantially affects interstate commerce." This language indicates that Congress intended to exercise its commerce power, not its taxing power. Although in other places Obamacare specifically uses the word *tax*, the individual mandate provision uses the word *penalty*. For example, Obamacare uses the *t* word in imposing new taxes on medical devices, indoor tanning services, and Cadillac health plans, and in raising new Medicare taxes for people making more than a certain income. The failure to call something a tax in one portion of the statute while calling something else a tax in another portion of the same statute is a strong indication of congressional intent to draw distinctions between the two. Congress clearly knew how to call a tax a tax when it wanted to.

The Obama administration argued that because the individual mandate section's penalty was placed in the Internal Revenue Code's section "Miscellaneous Excise Taxes," it should be considered a tax. But both Supreme Court precedent as well as the Internal Revenue Code itself says that the mere placement of something in the tax code should not create any "inference, implication or presumption" that Congress intended the provision to be a tax. Moreover, because Obamacare specifically divorced the individual mandate's penalty from Internal Revenue Service enforcement and collection methods – such as criminal proceedings, liens, and levies – this reinforces the overall impression that Congress didn't intend to enforce the individual mandate using its taxing power.

Courts also consider whether the exaction appears to be a revenue-generating measure that supports the government's functions. Taxes, in other words, are inherently designed to raise money to carry out programs in support of the general welfare. They're designed and intended to help carry out the government's business. Under Obamacare, there are seventeen specific items in a section called "Revenue Offset Provisions." There are several more in a section called

"Provisions Relating to Revenue." The individual mandate, however, isn't listed in either of these sections.

And finally, courts consider extrinsic evidence such as prior versions of the law. This, too, proves damaging to conceptualizing the mandate as an exercise of the taxing power. Prior versions of Obamacare passed by both the House and the Senate contained an individual mandate and specifically said noncompliance would result in the imposition of a tax. It wasn't until the final version, passed by the Senate on Christmas Eve 2009, that the word *tax* was replaced with the word *penalty*. This strongly suggests that Congress intentionally substituted words.

In light of all these relevant legal considerations, every court that has thus far considered the Obama administration's alternative taxing-power justification for the individual mandate has rejected it. And on a purely pragmatic level, there's something disturbing about the administration's attempt to switch constitutional power sources under the particular circumstances surrounding enactment of Obamacare. Supporters of Obamacare adamantly denied that the new law would increase taxes but would, instead, reduce the budget deficit.

In a highly publicized interview with CNN's George Stephanopoulos in September 2009, President Obama stridently denied that the individual mandate was enforced by a tax. When Stephanopoulos queried, "Under this mandate, the government is forcing people to spend money, fining you if you don't. How is that not a tax?" President Obama avoided responding by shifting the discussion to the costs of uncompensated care. Stephanopoulos interjected, "That may be, but it's still a tax increase," to which Obama replied, "No. That's not true, George." After more discussion about the costs of uncompensated care, Stephanopoulos quoted

Merriam Webster's definition of *tax* to Obama. Visibly angered, Obama shot back, "George, the fact that you looked up Merriam's Dictionary, the definition of tax increase, indicates to me that you're stretching a little bit right now. Otherwise, you wouldn't have gone to the dictionary to check on the definition." Stephanopoulos countered, "I wanted to check for myself. But your critics say it is a tax increase." Obama retorted, "My critics say everything is a tax increase." The discussion ended when Stephanopoulos asked, "But you reject that it's a tax increase?" and Obama responded, "I absolutely reject that notion."

It's clear that neither President Obama nor supporters of his health-reform bill wanted to use the *t* word, fearing the political consequences. Obama repeatedly assured Americans that his reform plan wouldn't increase taxes for anyone making less than $250,000 a year. Appearing on *Face the Nation* in September 2009, President Obama reiterated his campaign pledge not to raise taxes, proclaiming, "I can still keep that promise because, as I've said, about two-thirds of what we've proposed [in health-care reform] would be from money that's already in the healthcare system but is just being spent badly. And as I've said before, this is not me making wild assertions." By substituting the word *penalty* for the word *tax*, Congress avoided enacting a law that, on its face, contradicted the president's assurances to the American people.

None of Obamacare's supporters, from the president on down, wanted to admit that they were going to tax people for failing to buy health insurance. In an elaborate effort to avoid the *t* word, Obamacare supporters boxed themselves into a legal corner. Although there may have been a secret intent to impose taxes – and thus exercise the taxing power – courts can't base their decisions on legislators' secret intentions.

Congress said it was imposing a penalty and treated this exaction differently from other identified taxes. If it walks like a penalty and quacks like a penalty, it's a penalty.

C. FEDERALISM

The other constitutional challenge to Obamacare raised by the lawsuits doesn't have anything to do with the individual mandate. Instead, it focuses on Obamacare's expansion of Medicaid, the health-care program for the poor. The twenty-six states that have joined the Florida lawsuit argue that Obamacare's method of expanding Medicaid effectively "commandeers" the states, treating them like a junior partner to the federal government. It does this by putting states to a very unattractive Hobson's choice: either implement very expensive and administratively complex new Medicaid rules or opt out of Medicaid altogether, an option that would leave millions of poor Americans without any health insurance.

First, a little background about Medicaid is in order. Medicaid is a program administered jointly by the federal and state governments. The federal government sets minimum standards, and states decide whether to operate a Medicaid program. If a state opts to run a Medicaid program, the federal government matches state dollars spent. There's some variation from state to state, but in general, the federal government matches state Medicaid expenditures on a dollar-for-dollar basis. Accordingly, the costs of Medicaid – about $380 billion per year before Obamacare – are split roughly fifty-fifty between the federal and state governments. Even with federal matching dollars, Medicaid is the single largest item in state budgets, consuming about 21 percent of total state expenditures.

States have primary responsibility for running their Medicaid programs on a day-to-day basis, determining what income limitations apply, who qualifies for benefits, what optional benefits are available (above and beyond the minimum benefits set by federal law), and which providers are eligible to serve Medicaid patients.

Under Obamacare, Medicaid changes significantly. For the first time, the federal government will require that states cover all individuals under age sixty-five, whose incomes are at or below 133 percent of the federal poverty level. This is estimated to add about 20 million more people to Medicaid nationwide, about a 30 percent increase. The federal government will fund most of the cost of this expansion initially, but the states' proportion of cost sharing increases significantly in later years. For most states, the cost of this change alone amounts to billions of dollars per year.

Obamacare also increases reimbursement rates for certain kinds of doctors; alters the states' share of rebates from drug companies; and requires states to establish reinsurance programs, premium-rate review processes, and state insurance exchanges in which citizens can comparison shop for health insurance policies. States are permitted to opt out of operating their own insurance exchange, but if they do, it comes at a price: the federal government will take over operation of the exchange in the state, displacing the state's traditional police power to regulate health insurance.

The constitutional basis for the states' concerns about the impact of Medicaid expansion is the principle of federalism, or dual sovereignty. In the words of the Supreme Court in

New York v. United States (1992), "States are not mere political subdivisions of the United States. State governments are neither regional offices nor administrative agencies of the Federal Government. The positions occupied by state officials appear nowhere on the Federal Government's most detailed organizational chart. The Constitution instead 'leaves to the several States a residuary and inviolable sovereignty,' reserved explicitly to the States by the Tenth Amendment."

New York v. United States is the most important case defining what the principle of federalism protects. Although a series of Supreme Court decisions has effectively gutted much of the Tenth Amendment, one core idea remains, exemplified by the Court's decision in *New York* – namely, the anti-commandeering principle. Pursuant to this principle, the federal government can't "commandeer" the states to do the federal government's bidding. Because states aren't subsidiaries of the federal government, if the federal government wants to do X, the federal government must use its own resources and officers to accomplish X – it can't commandeer state officials to carry out federal law. This is why state police officers enforce state criminal law and federal law enforcement officials enforce federal criminal law. Likewise, state attorneys prosecute violations of state law, and federal attorneys prosecute violations of federal law. Each sovereign – the federal government plus each of the fifty states – operates in its own sphere.

The Florida Obamacare lawsuits assert that many provisions of health reform commandeer state officials. For example, states are required to establish and carry out a reinsurance program. They are required to collect data on the average risk of health insurance policies and assess a penalty (or reward) when insurers exceed (or undercut) the average. They also argue that, because expanding Medicaid eligibility to 133 percent of the federal poverty level dramatically increases the costs of running a Medicaid program, states are effectively forced to devote billions more dollars at a time when state budgets are stretched to capacity. Redirecting substantial sums of money to Medicaid, in turn, forces the states to cut back on other programs such as education and law enforcement.

In theory, states remain free, post-Obamacare, to discontinue their Medicaid programs altogether. The Supreme Court has repeatedly made it clear that Medicaid is a voluntary program. The states challenging Obamacare, however, assert that so many of their citizens have become dependent on Medicaid that opting out of the program would "desert millions of their residents, leaving them without access to the healthcare services they have depended on for decades under Medicaid." As a result, they claim, "States are forced to accept the harmful effects of the Act on their fiscs and their sovereignty."

There is some support for the states' novel argument. Although states' ability to opt out of Medicaid would normally dispose of a commandeering claim, the Supreme Court's decision in *South Dakota v. Dole* (1987) reinvigorates the claim to a certain degree. In *Dole*, the Supreme Court was asked to assess the constitutionality of a federal law that withheld 5 percent of federal highway funds in those states that failed to raise their drinking age to twenty-one. South Dakota, which allowed nineteen-year-olds to drink 3.2 percent beer, lost 5 percent of its federal highway dollars as a result of the law and challenged it as exceeding Congress's spending power.

The Supreme Court in *Dole* ruled in favor of the federal government, concluding that in spending its tax revenues, the federal government was free to "attach conditions on the receipt of federal funds." The Court articulated a four-part test for assessing the constitutionality of any strings attached to the receipt of federal money: (1) they must be in pursuit of the general welfare; (2) they must be unambiguously articulated; (3) they must be related to the government's interest in spending its money; and (4) they must not violate any other constitutional provisions.

After finding that the federal law in question satisfied all four of these factors, the *Dole* Court stated that in some circumstances, "financial inducement offered by Congress might be so coercive as to pass the point at which 'pressure turns into compulsion.'" It suggested that, when this imaginary line is crossed, an exercise of the spending power would be invalid. Such coercion was not present in the facts of *Dole* itself, however, because losing 5 percent of highway funds – a "relatively mild encouragement" – made any coercion argument "more rhetoric than fact."

Dole suggests that in a future case, strings attached by the federal government to the receipt of federal funds might cross the line from acceptable "encouragement" to unacceptable "coercion." The states challenging health reform assert that the law's mandatory Medicaid expansion crosses that line. It puts states to a Hobson's choice of either opting out of Medicaid entirely (thus avoiding all the new, expensive Medicaid strings) or abiding by the strings and incurring billions of dollars in cost-sharing liabilities they can't afford. Either way, the argument goes, the reform law's Medicaid expansion treats the states with a degree of disrespect unacceptable in a system of dual sovereignty. The federal government shouldn't be permitted to create a program under its spending power, lure the states into participating by providing a generous federal matching rate, and then change the rules of the program so dramatically that states can't afford to implement those rules.

The practical reality of Medicaid dependency for millions of people suggests something disturbingly dangerous to federalism is afoot. The bloated federal government collects massive tax revenues, which are showered on states through exercises of the federal spending power. States lap up these federal dollars like thirsty dogs and, over time, have become dependent on the largesse of their federal master to prevent dehydration. Although the states are theoretically free to turn off the federal spigot, doing so would mean financial suicide for many.

In essence, therefore, the states challenging Obamacare are making a federalism argument, based on the same notion of respect for state sovereignty embodied by the anti-commandeering principle. But because states can technically opt out of Medicaid, the only available precedent embodying respect for federalism that is available is the dicta from *South Dakota v. Dole* about the possibility of a future case presenting sufficient facts to constitute coercion.

Although no coercion was found in *Dole*, the case involved a withholding of only 5 percent of federal highway funds. In the case of Obamacare's Medicaid expansion, states that refuse to play by federal rules don't lose 5 percent of Medicaid dollars; they lose all Medicaid dollars. This is obviously much more significant than in *Dole*, thus bolstering the coercion claim.

Lower federal courts that have been asked to consider *Dole*-based coercion claims in other contexts have uniformly rejected them. Coercion claims aren't getting traction for the simple reason that the Supreme Court in *Dole* provided no guidance about how to know when federal strings cross the line from encouragement to coercion. Does coercion depend on the percentage of federal funds cut off? Or perhaps the percentage of total expenditures is lost when federal dollars dry up? Or maybe it matters whether alternative sources of funding are available, such as state income taxes or charitable contributions? As one U.S. Court of Appeals put it, "[C]an a sovereign state which is always free to increase its tax revenues ever be coerced by the withholding of federal funds – or is the state merely presented with hard political choices?"

Because there's no case law allowing lower courts to apply a coercion theory, they cannot be expected to rule in favor of this federalism-based challenge to health reform. Even Judge Vinson in the Florida case – who ruled in favor of the states on their Commerce Clause arguments – refused to nibble on the coercion claim. He concluded: "I appreciate the difficult situation in which the states find themselves. It is a matter of historical fact that at the time the Constitution was drafted and ratified, the Founders did not expect that the federal government would be able to provide sizeable funding to the states and, consequently, be able to exert power over the states to the extent that it currently does.... Some have suggested that, in the interest of federalism, the Supreme Court should revisit and reconsider its Spending Clause cases. However, unless and until that happens, the states have little recourse to remaining the very junior partner in this partnership." This really says it all: The only way the federalism-based coercion argument can succeed is at the Supreme Court level. Until then, expect failure on this particular challenge to Obamacare.

As this chapter has shown, contrary to the political left's assertion, the lawsuits challenging Obamacare are far from frivolous. They raise serious and legitimate constitutional concerns, particularly relating to the reach of the Commerce

Clause and the relationship between federalism and the congressional spending power. The constitutional questions posed by health reform are critically important to the principle of limited government. If the law is sustained, there won't be much of this principle remaining. Tea Partiers understand that the stakes are high with health reform. Their persistent objection to it isn't based on racism, a desire to turn back the clock, disdain for the Democrat Party, or support for the Republican Party. It's based on the principle of limited government, a uniquely American principle worthy of study and reverence by all, regardless of political affiliation.

☆ 3 ☆

U.S. Sovereignty

T HE SECOND DEFINING PRINCIPLE OF THE TEA
Party is its unapologetic defense of U.S. sovereignty.
Tea Partiers believe that the United States has a
right and a duty to defend its geographic territory and legal
independence from other nations and supranational entities
such as the United Nations. The sovereignty principle is evident in several issues of importance to the Tea Party, including the war on terror, immigration, and the role of international
law in applying and interpreting the U.S. Constitution. Before
diving into these controversies, however, it's useful to discuss
what sovereignty means, why the Tea Party thinks it's so
important, and what could happen if it's lost.

In its most basic sense, sovereignty is power. Power over
what? The power to make, interpret, and enforce law. This is
why God is often referred to as a sovereign, because Christians
and Jews believe he made, and judges compliance with, the
Ten Commandments. In secular terms, sovereignty is concerned with man-made laws that are understood and acqui-
esced to within a specific geographic territory. In any given
geographic area, the people residing there will recognize a

person or group of persons with the power to make, interpret, and enforce law. This sovereignty may be parsed among multiple people or entities, each with limited and defined spheres of power. In the United States, for example, the Constitution divides sovereignty between a law-making branch (Congress), a law-executing branch (the president), and a law-interpreting branch (courts). Each of these branches has a share of sovereignty, but none possesses the whole of it. Dividing sovereignty horizontally, among various branches of government, is one way to check against tyranny.

As discussed in the previous chapter, the U.S. Constitution also divides sovereignty vertically, between the federal and state governments. The federal government was given only limited, enumerated powers, and the remainder were reserved – in the words of the Tenth Amendment – "to the States respectively, or to the people." This vertical separation of powers – referred to as federalism – is another critical architectural feature designed to prevent the abuse of sovereign power. And even within the federal and state sovereigns' respective spheres of power, the Constitution cordons off areas of no power – that is to say, individual rights – in which governments cannot act. Governments presumptively cannot, for example, infringe individuals' liberty to speak, exercise religion, or keep and bear arms. All these elaborate and purposeful constitutional limits on – and divisions of – sovereignty were devised with one overarching goal in mind: checking tyranny.

Globalism moves in the opposite direction envisioned by the U.S. Constitution. Instead of dividing and subdividing sovereignty among different branches and levels of government, globalism seeks consolidation. This explains why globalists view the Constitution with disdain – it's an annoying impediment to accomplishing their goals. As globalist government professor James MacGregor Burns candidly observed: "Let us face reality. The framers have simply been too shrewd for us. They have outwitted us. They designed separated institutions that cannot be unified by mechanical linkages, frail bridges, tinkering. If we are to 'turn the founders upside down' – to put together what they put asunder – we must directly confront the Constitutional structure they erected." This chapter explores the various ways in which internationalists are trying to "turn the founders upside down" and "put together what they put asunder."

One of the chief difficulties with criticizing internationalism is that, at least on its surface, its goals seem so beneficent. It aims to improve human rights and the standard of living of the poor. But achieving these goals – even assuming they can be defined and accurately measured – cannot be accomplished satisfactorily to most internationalists if they are merely precatory. Globalists aren't aiming to expand charitable giving or to educate, recognize, and enforce individuals' natural rights against government interference – quite the opposite. They aim to bulk up government, making it bigger and stronger, using global sovereignty as a means to enforce certain norms or values that are only vaguely defined. As with all exercises of sovereignty – globalists insist that these values be enforceable, because laws without sanctions are understandably ignored when it's convenient to do so. The internationalists' agenda is to globalize sovereignty itself, consolidating power to make, interpret, and enforce laws they deem desirable.

To some, talk about one world government seems like paranoid, conspiratorial science fiction. To others, global sovereignty is pragmatically possible, normatively desirable, and perhaps even inevitable. Tea Partiers fall between these extremes. They recognize that there's an organized, earnest, and increasingly successful push toward internationalism. Yet they vigorously oppose the internationalist agenda for one simple reason: it's inconsistent with the Constitution and, consequently, not in the best interests of U.S. citizens.

Although it may seem obvious that every country has the right to make and enforce its own laws, many academics – and virtually all lawyers who teach or practice international law – believe the traditional, territorially limited conception of sovereignty is outdated. As David Brooks recently confessed in a *New York Times* op-ed, the "educated class is internationalist." Indeed, in my own law school – housed in a university with the word *international* in its name – there's great pride in the fact that every class requires a certain number of hours of instruction on international or comparative law. This instruction is rarely critical of internationalism. Instead, internationalism is enthusiastically embraced as critically important, ineluctable, and superior to old-fashioned territorial sovereignty.

Although exposure to international or comparative laws may be useful in certain contexts, providing perspective isn't really the goal of the internationalists. There's a dark underbelly to internationalism that's rarely acknowledged by its votaries, and even more rarely understood by the impressionable young minds who sit through lecture after lecture touting its wonders. Many ardent internationalists are motivated by a desire to restrict the power and redistribute the wealth of certain countries, particularly the United States. Consider carefully the words of President Obama in his speech to Cairo University in the summer of 2009: "Given our interdependence, any world order that elevates one nation or group of people over another will inevitably fail. So whatever we think of the past, we must not be prisoners to it. Our problems must be dealt with through partnership, our progress must be shared." This view of internationalism – that the United States shouldn't try to "elevate" itself above other countries, should deal with its problems "through partnership" and should "share" its progress – is one of the most dangerous long-term threats to our country. At its core, it indicates a desire to reign in U.S. power and redistribute U.S. wealth to less affluent parts of the world.

Tea Partiers aren't intimidated by insinuations that rejecting globalism is antediluvian, arrogant, or protectionist. They understand its dark side, as evidenced by their hostility toward the United Nations. For example, the Maine Republican Party, led by Tea Party activists, adopted a party platform in May 2010 that declares opposition to "any and all treaties with the U.N. or any other organization or country which surrenders U.S. sovereignty." Likewise, Senator Rand Paul of Kentucky has asserted that the United Nations "has become a forum for dictators like Hugo Chavez of Venezuela and Muamar el Gadafi of Libya to insult the United States." Congressman Ron Paul has repeatedly introduced a bill, the American Sovereignty Restoration Act, which would withdraw the United States from the United Nations entirely. Most recently, Republican Congresswoman Ileana Ros-Lehtinen of Florida, the new chair of the House Foreign Relations Committee, declared in a March 2011 *Miami Herald* op-ed that "it is clear that the UN is broken." She argued that the United States should withdraw from the UN Human Rights Council because it's a "sham" dominated by "serial human rights abusers" such as China, Cuba, Libya, Russia, Saudi Arabia, and Syria, and that UN contributions should become voluntary because its agenda too often fails to "advance our interests and our values." Such low opinions aren't held only by Republicans and members of the Tea Party. A poll conducted by Gallup in February 2010 revealed that less than a third (31 percent) of Americans think the United Nations is doing a "good job" in "trying to solve the problems it has had to face."

Whatever one thinks about the virtues or vices of the United Nations and internationalism in general, it's important to acknowledge that the debate about internationalism isn't a debate about whether sovereignty itself is a good idea. Short of a utopian state of anarchy – in which people live peacefully without the need for any laws imposed and enforced by a sovereign – the recognition of a sovereign is inevitable, given human nature. And this is a good thing, too: sovereignty brings stability and accountability to a society. The chaos inherent in anarchy – the so-called state of nature pondered by philosophers such as Thomas Hobbes and John Locke – is replaced with a relatively stable set of laws that enable the citizenry to plan and prosper. People know who's responsible for making, enforcing, and interpreting the laws, and the holders of sovereign power are accordingly accountable to the people. So the question isn't about whether, but about how big, a sovereign should be. After all, both national and global sovereigns are sovereigns. In either case, there's a recognized government that makes, enforces, and interprets law.

So what advantage is there in sticking with traditional, territorially divided sovereigns as opposed to embracing, at least in some circumstances, a global sovereign? The answer lies in the U.S. Constitution itself. Remember that the founders were adamant in their belief that a divided sovereign was better than a unitary one. They understood that the risk of tyranny is reduced when there are multiple sovereign actors, all of which wield only a specific portion of sovereignty. Each of these sovereign actors, in turn, is accountable to the people for how it wields its power and consequently must compete for the affection of the people.

Globalizing any aspect of sovereignty undermines this principle. If there's only one global entity that wields all, or even a portion, of sovereignty, it has no need to compete for the affection of the people. There's no competition. A global sovereign may be accountable to the people in some way (perhaps through periodic elections), but the lack of competition reduces the degree and constancy of its incentive to be accountable.

Let's take a simple example involving criminal law. Various sovereigns around the globe – including the United States – presently wield the power to make, enforce, and interpret their own criminal laws. Within the United States, sovereignty over criminal law is subdivided among the federal government, fifty state governments, and various territories. This division is very beneficial to people of the United States. Let's assume that your loved one becomes terminally ill. The illness causes its sufferers to become highly dependent on caregivers and causes great pain. Your loved one would like to have some control over her future and obtain a physician's assistance with dying.

When sovereignty over criminal law is divided territorially, you'll likely have some choices. Several nations and U.S. states permit physician-assisted suicide, whereas other sovereigns consider it a crime. Having different sovereigns provides you with meaningful choice, thus affecting individual liberty in very real and meaningful ways. If only one global entity was given power to make, enforce, and interpret criminal law, there'd be no choice at all – and hence, no liberty – if that monolithic sovereign criminalized physician-assisted suicide. Competition among sovereigns is thus similar to competition among businesses – in both instances, competition expands freedom of choice.

Having multiple sovereigns creates multiple approaches to legal issues. Each sovereign is its own unique legal laboratory, allowing citizens to experiment with solutions that seem best suited to their own particular culture. A global, one-size-fits-all sovereignty doesn't allow for such variation. The net result is stifled innovation and, in the long term, an inability even to imagine different approaches to solving problems. The ability of nations and peoples "to be different" is a critically important dimension of human liberty that should be exalted, not expunged.

One need look no further than the European Union for a good example of what can happen when citizens trade in traditional territorial sovereignty for a larger, supranational sovereignty. In the European Union, twenty-seven nations have ceded significant portions of their sovereignty to an entity with binding authority over them. The European Union's institutions have exclusive or supreme power – even supreme to national constitutions – in several important areas such as trade, commerce, monetary policy, agriculture, environmental and energy policy, consumer protection, public health, and some aspects of social policy. The European Union's elaborate structure – far too complex to fully detail in this book – includes numerous giant administrative agencies, a multilevel court system, a central bank, the Council of Ministers, the European Council, and the European Parliament.

Why has Europe done this? Why have nations such as France and Germany relinquished so much of their sovereignty to a monolithic European Union? The answer lies in history. The history of the continent of Europe has been replete with empires – the long-lasting Roman Empire (both East and West), the Napoleonic Empire, the German Third Reich. And for at least brief periods, such empires ushered in periods of relative peace across the continent. Successful empires can unite disparate peoples and impose peace, even if by force.

Europeans seem to yearn for peace in a way unknown to Americans. And they seem to associate empires with peace. From the European perspective, what better way to prevent future pan-European or even global wars than to build a pan-European or global empire that will impose peace? Unity equals peace. In this way, unity indeed is the price one must pay for peace. If variation – freedom – is lessened or even eradicated, this is acceptable, so long as the end result is peace.

Americans obviously look at things differently than the Europeans. Indeed, in some ways the American view of peace is diametrically opposed to that of Europe. Americans believe that peace is important, of course, but that peace often can be achieved only by conflict and even war. Conflict, not unity, often equals peace. What's valued in the American tradition isn't unity but rugged individualism. Individual freedom takes priority over communitarian unity. This also helps explain the deep – and uniquely American – disdain and distrust of communism, something Europeans don't share, as evidenced by the relative electoral success of communist parties in various European parliaments.

European nations' relinquishment of sovereignty to the European Union is thus understandable from a historical perspective. Europeans view large-scale, governmentally imposed unity as the best way to achieve peace. A supra-national structure such as the European Union is believed to facilitate peace by providing a unitary decision-making structure to harmonize different cultural, ethnic, religious and political viewpoints. To Americans, such a unitary approach smacks of a least-common-denominator compromise that squelches individuality, experimentation, and excellence.

Supranational sovereign structures such as the European Union do offer efficiencies of scale and reduce balkanization. But they also inherently create a "democratic deficit" for the people residing in them. The European Union has created a massive political shift away from the elected parliaments of member states to the executive and administrative bureau-cracies of the European Union itself. The net result is that people in EU countries have less ability to influence policies and laws that affect their daily lives. Their own parliaments are gradually becoming empty shells, devoid of real sovereign power.

The only directly politically accountable EU institution is the European Parliament (EP), the members of which are elected by citizens in individual EU nations. But the EP does very little to reduce the European Union's democratic deficit. The people of Europe don't have much understanding of, or even interest in, the EP, as evidenced by historically low voter turnout for EP elections. This disinterest is understandable, because the EP can't initiate any legislation (initiation belongs solely to the bureaucracy known as the European Commis-sion), its membership is rather large (capped at 751 members), and there aren't any cohesive pan-European political parties with which citizens can identify. Equally important, despite deepening legal integration, no real European identity has emerged. People living in the European Union still prefer to watch and participate in the goings-on of their own (increasingly impuissant) national parliaments, which are conducted in the local language and easier to meaningfully monitor.

The European Union's architecture has created a sovereign dominated by politically unaccountable bureaucrats. In a remarkable op-ed for the *Wall Street Journal* in March 2011, Daniel Hannan, a member of the European Parliament from Great Britain, warned Americans of becoming too enamored of all things European, reminding us, "The EU places supreme power in the hands of 27 unelected Commissioners invulnerable to public opinion. The will of the people is generally seen by Eurocrats as an obstacle to overcome, not a reason to change direction." Hannan asked, "Is a European future truly so terrible? Yes. I have been an elected member of the European Parliament for 11 years. I have seen firsthand what the European political model means. The critical difference between the American and European unions has to do with the location of power. The U.S. was founded on what we might loosely call the Jeffersonian ideal: the notion that decisions should be taken as closely as possible to the people they affect. The European Union was based on precisely the opposite ideal."

Some argue that the European Union's sovereign structure is analogous to – and thus has no more democratic deficit than – the federalist structure of the United States. But this is inaccurate. The European Union isn't a federalist government like the United States but instead a treaty-based organization. There's no central European constitution as there is in the United States. Although there was a major push to enact a European constitution shortly after the turn of the twenty-first century, it failed to win the required unanimous ratification when Dutch and French voters overwhelmingly rejected it in

2005 (subsequent referenda in the Czech Republic, Denmark, Ireland, Poland, Portugal, Sweden, and the United Kingdom were called off).

More important, both the state and federal governments in the United States are deeply politically accountable to the people, with at least two out of three branches of government (executive and legislative) sitting for elections on a regular basis. In many states, even the judges are elected as well. Unlike the European Parliament, these politically accountable branches in the United States wield substantial power; have clearly defined political parties; and are monitored very closely by the media, special-interest groups, and individual citizens. Democratic participation in the U.S. political branches is thus proportionate to their immense power.

The political accountability of the European Union, by contrast, is minimal. The European Union's democratic deficit – and arguably its downright disdain for democracy – is exemplified by the Treaty of Lisbon, which became effective in December 2009. The treaty did many things, including transferring significantly more power away from individual EU nations and to the European Union. It also took the substance of the European Constitution – which had been rejected by European voters in national referenda – and repackaged it into treaty form. Repackaging the European Constitution as a treaty allowed European elites supporting it – a group of high-level European politicians known as the Amato Group – to legally bypass the use of referenda in most countries, including the Netherlands and France, which had earlier rejected the constitution. Under the laws of most EU nations, treaties can be approved by a simple vote of parliament; they do not have to be voted on by the people via referendum.

The only EU country that held a referendum on the Treaty of Lisbon was Ireland, whose own constitution wouldn't permit approval by its parliament. In 2008, the Irish people rejected the treaty. But after all parliaments of the other EU member states approved the treaty, the Irish people faced tremendous pressure to reconsider. In a second referendum held in 2009, the Irish reversed, approving the treaty and allowing it to enter into force.

Using the treaty process to achieve the legal reforms envisioned by the rejected European Constitution is deeply troubling. It was designed specifically to bypass individual citizens by going directly to parliaments instead. And although members of Parliament are elected and hence, politically accountable to their constituents on election day, substituting parliamentary approval because referenda don't yield the "right" result in the eyes of the political elite reinforces the belief that democracy isn't highly valued in the European Union, at least not among European political elites. Within only a matter of months after the Dutch and French rejections of the European Constitution, the political elites were scheming to devise ways to dispense with popular democratic input. They calculated (successfully) that members of parliaments would be more amenable, less suspicious of the proposed major reforms. Perhaps this was because members of Parliament were more sophisticated or educated or persuadable than ordinary citizens. Perhaps members of Parliament supported the treaty because they thought they could convince constituents to reelect them on the basis of other issues, or simply because they believed the treaty's benefits outweighed its burdens, which would become apparent to constituents with time. Whatever the case may be, it's patent that obtaining the direct consent of the people of Europe was viewed as something that needed to be avoided at all costs, evidence of a deep disdain for democracy on critically important European legal reforms.

A. The Role of International Law in U.S. Constitutional Law

Could the same thing happening in Europe happen in the United States? Could the United States cede its sovereignty to some pan-American or global sovereign in the same way? To answer these questions, we have to look closely at both international law and the U.S. Constitution.

There are several provisions in the U.S. Constitution that relate to international law. In Article I, section 8, Congress is given the power to "define and punish . . . offenses against the law of nations." The "law of nations" refers to what is loosely called international law today, although at the time, the law of nations was much narrower in scope than modern international law. Specifically, the law of nations related to a code of conduct between nations, in which each sovereign was considered a coequal with other sovereigns, entitled to respect. Sovereigns were bound by a harm principle, or golden rule, by which they couldn't commit acts of aggression against other sovereigns unless in self-defense. Sovereigns could also enter into contracts with one another – called treaties – in which they agreed to abide by certain rules regarding one another's citizens, businesses (e.g., commerce, trade), or other external affairs.

In addition to this brief recognition of a power to legislate to punish offenses against the law of nations, the Constitution contains two additional important provisions relating to the power to make and enforce treaties. Article II, section 2, indicates that the president has the power "by and with the advice and consent of the Senate, to make treaties, provided two thirds of the senators present concur." Article VI – the Supremacy Clause – then reads: "This Constitution, and the laws of the United States which shall be made in pursuance thereof; and all treaties made, or which shall be made, under the authority of the United States, shall be the supreme law of the land; and the Judges in every State shall be bound thereby, anything in the Constitution or laws of any State to the contrary notwithstanding." Taken together, these two provisions allow treaties to be made by the president with the "advice and consent" of two-thirds of the Senate present, and then deem such treaties to be "supreme law of the land" if they are made "under the authority of the United States."

In *Federalist No. 75*, Alexander Hamilton explained to the American people why the treaty power was divided between the president and the Senate as follows:

> The essence of the legislative authority is to enact laws, or, in other words, to prescribe rules for the regulation of the society; while the execution of the laws, and the employment of the common strength, either for this purpose or for the common defense, seem to comprise all the functions of the executive magistrate. The power of making treaties is, plainly, neither the one nor the other. It relates neither to the execution of the subsisting laws, nor to the enaction of new ones; and still less to an exertion of the common strength. Its objects are CONTRACTS [caps in original] with foreign nations, which have the force of law, but derive it from the obligations of good faith. They are not rules prescribed by the sovereign to the subject, but agreements between sovereign and

sovereign. The power in question seems therefore to form a distinct department, and to belong, properly, neither to the legislative nor to the executive.

It's apparent from Hamilton's exegesis that treaties don't fit comfortably in the category of legislation. Legislation "prescribe[s] rules for the regulation of the society" in the sense that it directly affects the sovereign's subjects (citizens). Treaties, by contrast, are described as contracts made "between sovereign and sovereign" that don't prescribe general rules for a particular sovereign's citizens. In a very general sense, treaties regulated external acts of a nation in its relationship with other nations, whereas legislation (ordinary laws) regulated internal acts of a nation's citizens.

This was legal understanding of the treaty power until after World War II, when the United Nations was formed. Immediately after its creation, the United Nations and its branches began, in the words of Senator Everett Dirksen of Illinois, "grinding out treaties like so many eager beavers." The pace and unusual nature of this activity triggered alarms in the legal community by the early 1950s. There were two principal fears that emerged: (1) treaties were being used to undermine or contradict the U.S. Constitution, and (2) treaties were being used to govern internal domestic conduct rather than external relations between sovereigns.

With regard to the first fear – that treaties were being used to undermine the Constitution – the concern emanated from ambiguity in the constitutional text and Supreme Court case law. Article VI's Supremacy Clause requires federal statutes to be "made in pursuance" of the Constitution, but it uses very different language when declaring the supremacy of treaties, requiring for their supremacy only that they be made "under the authority of the United States." For a treaty to be made "under the authority of the United States," it need be agreed to only by the president and two-thirds of senators present. As a textual matter, therefore, Article VI implies that treaties do not have to be in pursuance of the Constitution.

This interpretation of the treaty power seemed to be confirmed by the Supreme Court's decision in *Missouri v. Holland* (1920). In *Missouri*, the Court ruled that Congress had constitutional power to pass a law implementing a treaty with Great Britain designed to protect migratory birds. This holding is unremarkable, except for the fact that the Supreme Court had ruled only six years earlier, in 1914, that the exact kind of law was unconstitutional in the absence of a treaty. The Court thought that animals such as birds were property belonging to the states, so regulating their migration was one of the powers reserved to the states via the Tenth Amendment. But once the treaty had been signed with Great Britain, suddenly Congress had the power to regulate the birds using the Necessary and Proper Clause. Dissected carefully, the *Missouri v. Holland* decision implied that the treaty power allowed Congress to evade the Tenth Amendment, and potentially other provisions of the Constitution as well.

Fears that the treaty power could be used to undermine the Constitution were thus not unfounded paranoia. And given the rapid proliferation of treaties being proposed after World War II, fear about a runaway treaty power being used to subvert the Constitution itself lead to the introduction of a series of proposed constitutional amendments in the early 1950s, referred to generically as the Bricker Amendment, after the amendments' chief proponent, U.S. Senator John Bricker of Ohio. The thrust of the Bricker Amendment was to reverse the Supreme Court's decision in *Missouri v. Holland*, declaring that treaties couldn't conflict with any part of the Constitution. The Bricker Amendment would have also clarified that no treaty could "become effective as internal law" unless both houses of Congress passed legislation authorizing such a domestic law.

In 1953, the Bricker Amendment came within one vote of passing the Senate by the two-thirds' required for proposing constitutional amendments. Although the Bricker Amendment failed, its broad support and attention to the issue created some pressure for the Supreme Court to take matters into its own hands. Just four years later, in 1957, the Court decided *Reid v. Covert*, a case involving a military prosecution of a serviceman's wife accused of murdering her husband. An executive agreement between the United States and the United Kingdom granted military courts exclusive jurisdiction to try such offenses committed by members of the military or their dependents while present in Great Britain. The Supreme Court ruled that the executive agreement was unconstitutional, violating American civilians' right to trial by jury in criminal cases. The Court's plurality opinion, penned by Justice Hugo Black, declared:

> There is nothing in [the Constitution] which intimates that treaties and laws enacted pursuant to [it] do not have to comply with the provisions of the Constitution.... It would be manifestly contrary to the objectives of those who created the Constitution, as well as those who were responsible for the Bill of Rights – let alone alien to our entire constitutional history and tradition – to construe Article VI as permitting the United States to exercise power under an international agreement without observing constitutional prohibitions. In

effect, such construction would permit amendment of that document in a manner not sanctioned by Article V.

Reid v. Covert finally put to bed the notion that treaties could undermine or disregard the Constitution itself. But worries still remain. The other critical component of the Bricker Amendment – halting the use of treaty law to affect domestic law affecting the behavior of U.S. citizens – has not been resolved. Treaties' tentacles have continued to reach deeper and deeper into U.S. domestic affairs since *Reid* was decided. Treaty law's principal focus has morphed from sovereign-to-sovereign contracts to sovereign-to-citizen rules affecting property, crimes, torts, domestic relations, and human rights. Secretary of State John Foster Dulles warned of a "trend toward trying to use the treatymaking power to effect internal social changes." Similarly, Frank Holman – a future president of the American Bar Association – wrote in the *American Bar Journal* in 1950, "Certainly until recently, to the average lawyer, it would have seemed unthinkable that the treatymaking power of the Federal Government could to any large extent be used to make domestic or local law for the people of the various states, and fantastic, that through the treatymaking power, state and federal legislative processes and judicial processes could be by-passed by a group of internationalists sitting in a committee-room of the United Nations and formulating treaties, conventions and covenants for successive ratification."

In 1965, the Second Restatement of Foreign Relations Law – a document drafted by expert lawyers to restate the current state of U.S. international law – recognized that a treaty is constitutional only if it involves a "matter [that] is of international concern." By 1987, however, the Third Restatement of Foreign Relations Law was formulated; it reversed this historical understanding 180 degrees. The Third Restatement proclaims: "Contrary to what was once suggested, the Constitution does not require that an international agreement deal only with 'matters of international concern.' ... International law knows no limitations on the purpose or subject matter of international agreements.... [T]he United States may make an agreement on any subject suggested by its national interests in relations with other nations." The drafters of the Third Restatement cite no authority for this change in doctrine, nor any reason such a broad new understanding is needed.

Discarding the internal-external affairs distinction is contrary to the original understanding of the treaty power. The treaty power enables the United States to enter into contracts with other nations as nations – in other words, agreements regarding how the United States will deal with the property and citizens of other nations while they're present within U.S. borders, as well as agreements relating to borders, the conduct of foreign relations, and the use of military force vis-à-vis other nations. We've come a very long way from Hamilton's assurance to the ratifying American public in *Federalist No. 75* that the treaty power's "objects are CONTRACTS [caps in original] with foreign nations, which have the force of law, but derive it from the obligations of good faith. They are not rules prescribed by the sovereign to the subject, but agreements between sovereign and sovereign." It is likewise contradictory of Madison's statement at the Virginia ratifying convention that "[t]he object of treaties is the regulation of intercourse with foreign nations and is external." And it is also contrary to Thomas Jefferson's assertion, "By the general power to make treaties, the Constitution must have intended to comprehend only those objects which are usually regulated by treaty, and cannot be otherwise regulated."

Acknowledging a boundless power to make treaties that directly regulate the behavior of U.S. citizens within U.S. borders is an open invitation to fundamentally change domestic U.S. law without the approval of both houses of Congress. If the president and two-thirds of U.S. senators present concur, a treaty can now change any aspect of domestic U.S. law.

To understand the breadth of this potential loss of U.S. sovereignty, let's examine one important international law example in detail – climate change. Those who advocate for tough laws to reduce global warming use dire predictions reminiscent of the Bible's book of Revelation. Consider a speech given by then-senator Barack Obama in 2006: "All across the world, in every kind of environment and region known to man, increasingly dangerous weather patterns and devastating storms are abruptly putting an end to the long-running debate over whether or not climate change is real. Not only is it real, it's here, and its effects are giving rise to a frighteningly new global phenomenon: the man-made natural disaster." Or former vice president Al Gore's remarks upon receiving the 2007 Nobel Peace Prize:

> We, the human species, are confronting a planetary emergency – a threat to the survival of our civilization that is gathering ominous and destructive potential even as we gather here.... [O]ur world is spinning out of kilter. Major cities... are nearly out of water due to massive droughts and melting glaciers. Desperate farmers are losing their livelihoods. Peoples in the frozen Arctic and on low-lying Pacific islands are planning evacuations

of places they have long called home. Unprecedented wildfires have forced a half million people from their homes in one country and caused a national emergency that almost brought down the government in another.... Stronger storms in the Pacific and Atlantic have threatened whole cities. Millions have been displaced by massive flooding in South Asia, Mexico, and 18 countries in Africa. As temperature extremes have increased, tens of thousands have lost their lives.

The globalists don't want to let a perceived good crisis go to waste. Assuming it's perceived as a crisis by people around the globe, global warming presents a perfect opportunity to implement the broader internationalist agenda. One of the most significant steps toward implementing that agenda occurred in 1997, with development of the Kyoto protocol. The Kyoto protocol is an amendment to the UN Framework Convention on Climate Change (UNFCCC), a treaty dealing with greenhouse-gas emissions such as carbon dioxide (CO_2). Under Kyoto, a group of countries – called Annex I countries – agreed to reduce their greenhouse-gas emissions by 5.2 percent by 2012. The Annex I countries' commitment is legally binding, although Kyoto gives them some limited flexibility to achieve the emissions reduction goal, including the use of a carbon-trading or cap-and-trade program. The European Union, for example, opted to use an elaborate cap-and-trade program, called the EU Emissions Trading Scheme.

Under a cap-and-trade system, greenhouse-gas emissions, particularly CO_2, are capped at a certain level, and emitters – such as power companies and other businesses – are allotted a certain number of carbon credits. If a business emits more carbon than the carbon credits allotted by the government, it must buy carbon credits or face a hefty penalty. Businesses that don't use all their carbon credits – because they find a way to reduce their carbon emissions somehow – can sell their excess carbon credits and make more money. The overall effect of a cap-and-trade regime, therefore, is to reward low carbon emitters and punish high emitters.

The United States has refused to ratify the Kyoto protocol. Although President Clinton initially signed Kyoto, the Senate unanimously rejected it, by a vote of 95–0. In a 2008 speech, then president George W. Bush explained why he and the U.S. Senate had opposed Kyoto:

> The Kyoto Protocol would have required the United States to drastically reduce greenhouse gas emissions. The impact of this agreement, however, would have been to limit our economic growth and to shift American jobs to other countries – while allowing major developing nations to increase their emissions. Countries like China and India are experiencing rapid economic growth – and that's good for their people and it's good for the world. This also means that they are emitting increasingly large quantities of greenhouse gases – which has consequences for the entire global climate.... The wrong way [to address global warming] is to unilaterally impose regulatory costs that put American businesses at a disadvantage with their competitors abroad – which would simply drive American jobs overseas and increase emissions there. The right way is to ensure that all major economies are bound to take action and to work cooperatively with our partners for a fair and effective international climate agreement.

Kyoto was the opening foray into carbon trading as a means to reduce greenhouse gases. Because Kyoto expired in 2012, discussions began almost immediately after Kyoto to replace it with something more ambitious. The UN-led discussions to replace Kyoto culminated in the UN Climate Change Conference held in Copenhagen, Denmark, in December 2009. After numerous preparatory conferences and rounds of discussion, it was widely believed that a new international treaty establishing strict and enforceable limits on greenhouse gases, particularly CO_2 emissions, would emerge from Copenhagen. Drafts circulated before Copenhagen aspired to establish a series of global organizations, under the auspices of the United Nations, to devise, monitor, and enforce a mandatory cap-and-trade regime.

Let's step back for a minute to consider what a mandatory cap-and-trade law would mean to average people. It punishes businesses that consume "too much" energy by making them buy carbon credits. This is just a hidden tax and, like all taxes, it will be passed along to consumers in form of higher prices. Under a cap-and-trade system, the price of everything goes up, because every good or service requires energy to produce. The price of energy itself will rise steeply, because the most prevalent energy-producing methods used today – such as coal plants – emit comparatively large quantities of greenhouse gases. People will consequently pay more to heat their houses, fuel their cars, cook their food, and clean their clothes. The price of all other goods and services will also climb – such as clothing, food, housing, cars, jewelry, and movies. Rising prices across all sectors of the economy will dampen the economy, as households can afford to buy fewer goods and services.

In a cap-and-trade economy, more money will be funneled into energy-saving sectors of the economy such as fluorescent light bulbs, electric cars, and solar panels, but these economic winners will be far outweighed by the other economic-sector losers. The net result is that energy becomes even more of a precious commodity than before cap-and-trade – more expensive and less readily available. Lights will get dimmer, houses will get colder in winter and hotter in summer, and cars will get smaller. In a very real sense, individuals' standard of living – at least in the world's developed countries – declines in meaningful and measurable ways.

Because of these concerns, an attempt to enact a cap-and-trade system in the United States failed in 2010. The Obama administration strongly supported cap-and-trade, and with Democrats in control of both the House and the Senate, a cap-and-trade proposal seemed destined to succeed. The main bill, called the Waxman-Markey bill, would have mandated an 83 percent reduction in greenhouse-gas emissions by 2050. It passed the House of Representatives in late June 2009, by a highly partisan vote of 219–212. The Senate, however, never took action.

Cap-and-trade failed in the Senate for many reasons. Chief among its problems was massive cost and concomitant effect on the already fragile U.S. economy. Although the Environmental Protection Agency estimated that the Waxman-Markey bill would increase costs to the average American household by only about $160 per year, other estimates pegged this number much higher. For example, a study of Waxman-Markey by the Heritage Foundation estimated that by 2035 (before full implementation), gasoline prices would rise 58 percent; natural gas prices would rise 55 percent; heating oil prices would rise 56 percent; and electricity prices would rise 90 percent. Including taxes, an average family of four would pay an additional $4,609 per year, and the United States would lose nearly 2.5 million jobs. Another study by the National Association of Manufacturers estimated that by 2030, Waxman-Markey would cause the loss of 1.8 million to 2.4 million U.S. jobs and would raise natural gas prices by up to 74 percent, electricity prices by up to 50 percent, and gasoline prices by up to 26 percent. Overall, by 2030, the National Association of Manufacturers study estimated that Waxman-Markey would lower the U.S. gross domestic product by an astounding 1.8 percent to 2.4 percent.

Opposition to Waxman-Markey in the Senate was also based on deep concerns about its potential impact on U.S. sovereignty. An editorial by the *Washington Examiner* in July 2009, for example, decried cap-and-trade legislation, asserting, "Obama has not hesitated to surrender U.S. sovereignty piecemeal to suit the global governance crowd. Yet this relish for global governance stops at the water's edge. The president hasn't demanded similar [cap and trade] action from India and China. And nobody seriously expects him to do so, ever. Global governance must not take precedent over American sovereignty." Although domestic cap-and-trade legislation wouldn't, standing alone, cede sovereignty to an international organization like the United Nations, it was widely believed that enactment of domestic legislation would have created great momentum for success at the Copenhagen climate change conference. John Podesta, president of the Center for American Progress, a liberal think tank, put it this way: "Without meaningful action in Congress, the Obama administration will lack the credibility to cajole developing nations to reduce their growing emissions as part of the Copenhagen global warming talks this December. The chance to adopt meaningful clean-energy and global warming policies will evaporate for at least two years."

The globalists' passion for an international cap-and-trade regime is understandable. Instituting an enforceable cap-and-trade regime on a global – rather than just domestic – level would enable global redistribution of wealth. Global cap-and-trade is extremely seductive for those whose goals extend beyond saving the planet. In a perverted way, climate change may enable the green movement to accomplish something the communist red movement never could – in Karl Marx's phraseology, "From each according to his ability, to each according to his needs!"

A global cap-and-trade treaty would be premised on the idea that wealthy countries owe a "climate debt" to the rest of the world that doesn't emit as much CO_2 because they aren't wealthy enough to own the cars, manufacturing and power plants, and other energy-consuming goods that emit CO_2. Climate debt is little more than repackaged reparations paid to poor countries, an expensive apology for having a vibrant economy that consumes a good deal of energy.

The wealth redistributionist agenda of global cap-and-trade is illustrated by progressive ethicist Peter Singer's statement in *One World*: "[S]ince the wealth of the developed nations is inextricably tied to their prodigious use of carbon fuels . . . it is a small step from here to the conclusion that the present global distribution of wealth is the result of the wrongful expropriation by a small fraction of the world's population of a resource that belongs to all human beings in common." This is also echoed in a 2009 book, *Climate Justice for a Changing Planet*, published by the UN Non-Governmental Liaison Service: "The concept of climate justice acknowledges that because the world's richest countries have contributed most to the problem, they have a greater obligation to take action and to do so more quickly. However, many fear that whatever international agreement is reached between governments, it will compound the already unjust burden on the poor and vulnerable. A rapidly growing number of social movements and civil society organizations across the world are mobilizing around this climate justice agenda."

Bolivia's ambassador to the United Nations, Pablo Solón, articulated the moral indignation of undeveloped countries in these graphic terms: "Admitting responsibility for the climate crisis without taking necessary actions to address it is like someone burning your house and then refusing to pay for it. Even if the fire was not started on purpose, the industrialized countries, through their inaction, have continued to add fuel to the fire.... It is entirely unjustifiable that countries like Bolivia are now forced to pay for the crisis. This creates a huge draw on our limited resources to protect our people from a crisis created by the rich and their over-consumption.... To us it seems only right that the polluter should pay, and not the poor.... As they say in the U.S., if you break it, you buy it."

Statements like these are common among global environmentalists. The wealth-redistribution aims of cap-and-trade aren't hidden. But talk about wealth redistribution doesn't have quite the same sex appeal as talk about justice and helping the poor. So the primary tactic of the global environmentalists is to use the phrase "climate justice," which, like any other movement with the word *justice* in it these days, is framed in terms of moral condemnation of wealthy capitalist nations' excesses, whose "greed" is harming – nay, killing – our less fortunate brothers and sisters around the globe. Venezuelan President Hugo Chávez gave a speech at the

Copenhagen conference that crackled with hostility toward capitalist nations:

> One could say . . . that a specter is haunting Copenhagen, to paraphrase Karl Marx, the great Karl Marx, a specter is haunting the streets of Copenhagen. . . . Capitalism is the specter, almost nobody wants to mention it. . . . The rich are destroying the planet. Do they think they can go to another when they destroy this one? Do they have plans to go to another planet? . . . We cannot reduce global material consumption if we don't make the powerful go down several levels, and if we don't combat inequality. . . . The political conservatism and selfishness of the largest consumers, of the richest countries shows high insensitivity and lack of solidarity with the poor, the hungry, and the most vulnerable to disease, to natural disasters.

The UN book *Climate Justice for a Changing Planet* directly linked climate change to certain death for the planet's vulnerable populations, proclaiming without blinking, "Already, it is estimated that fallout from climate change kills 300,000 people a year, including through the spread of disease and malnutrition, and seriously affects another 325 million. Four billion people are vulnerable in some fashion; 500 million are at extreme risk."

The validity of such doomsday scenarios are extremely difficult to assess, even for scientists. After having been told the sky is falling for years now, Americans – particularly Tea Partiers – seem to be concluding that global warming is more hype than horror. A poll by Rasmussen in fall 2010 showed that only 40 percent of Americans think global warming is attributable primarily to human activity, and a solid majority (59 percent) believe there's "significant disagreement" among scientists about the extent and causes of global warming. Similarly, a March 2011 Gallup poll revealed that a slim majority (51 percent) of Americans still feel a "great deal" or "fair amount" of "worry" over global warming, but 48 percent reported that their worry level was "not much" or "not at all." And tellingly, the ranks of the worriers are declining rather dramatically. Although worriers still slightly outnumber the nonworriers, the worrier category has declined by a substantial 12 percentage points over the past ten years.

Skepticism about global warming is even higher among Tea Partiers than the general public. An April 2010 poll by the *New York Times* and CBS News revealed that 51 percent of Tea Partiers believe global warming would have "no serious impact" on the environment, and an additional 15 percent think it "doesn't exist." By comparison, only 24 percent of non–Tea Partiers thought global warming would have "no serious impact," and only 5 percent thought it "doesn't exist."

These polls reflect the public's understanding that there isn't scientific agreement about (1) the existence of global warming; (2) human beings' responsibility for rising temperatures (as opposed to natural causes); or (3) the consequences of climate change, even assuming that number one is true. Although there does seem to be greater agreement regarding number one than numbers two or three, none of them is certain. And if any of these propositions is in reasonable doubt, implementation of a global cap-and-trade regime that will substantially affect developed countries' economies and massively redistribute their wealth makes zero sense.

As Lord Christopher Monckton, former science adviser to British Prime Minister Margaret Thatcher, said in a 2009 interview:

> The correct policy to address a non-problem is to have the courage to do nothing. However, they [the global environmentalists] are not concerned with whether there is a problem or not. They merely wish to pretend that there is a problem, and try to do so with a straight face, for long enough to persuade, not the population, because we have no say in this, but the governing class in the various member-states of the United Nations Framework on Climate Change: That they should hand over their powers as government to the United Nations. . . . So that we would no longer be free to decide what our currency would be, or how much of it there should be, or what we could burn, or what we could do. These things would be dictated to us by the dictators at the center. And this is an extremely dangerous moment, because it repudiates freedom, it repudiates democracy, and it denies us both of those.

Monckton was so alarmed by what could happen at Copenhagen that he went on a speaking tour in the United States, entreating America not to sign a global cap-and-trade treaty:

> [T]hank you, America. You *were* the beacon of freedom to the world. It is a privilege merely to stand on this soil of freedom – while it is still free. But in the next few weeks, unless you stop it – your President will sign your freedom, your democracy, and your prosperity away forever. And neither you, nor any subsequent government you may elect, will have any power whatsoever to take it

back again. That is how serious it is. . . . But I think it is here – here in your great nation . . . at this eleventh hour, at the fifty-ninth minute and the fifty-ninth second, you will rise up and you will stop your President from signing that dreadful treaty.

Fortunately, Monckton's warnings were heeded, and no treaty on cap-and-trade emerged from Copenhagen. What did emerge was a loose agreement initiated by the United States, China, India, Brazil, and South Africa to take unspecified steps to keep global temperature increases to less than two degrees Celsius. It also contained the statement, "In the context of meaningful mitigation actions and transparency on implementation, developed countries commit to a goal of mobilizing jointly USD 100 billion dollars a year by 2020 to address the needs of developing countries." This agreement – called the Copenhagen Accord – lacks treaty status and imposes no legally binding commitments.

Needless to say, the global environmentalists were deeply disappointed and pinned most of the blame on the United States. The Sudanese chief negotiator at Copenhagen for the so-called G77 group of developing nations claimed that the accord "is asking Africa to sign a suicide pact, an incineration pact in order to maintain the economic dependence of a few countries. It's a solution based on values that funneled six million people in Europe into furnaces." Analogizing the inability to achieve a global cap-and-trade treaty to the Holocaust is strong rhetoric, but much was at stake for the globalists in Copenhagen.

Copenhagen represented a critical test for the globalist agenda. Cap-and-trade was the perfect poster child for a "justice"-based movement to erode sovereignty and redistribute wealth. It reflected a sincerely held belief that countries such as the United States have no moral right to defend their own interests if doing so could, in the judgment of others, have possible negative consequences for anyone else on the planet.

If countries don't have a right to defend their own interests, they have no sovereignty. The very definition of sovereignty presupposes that the preeminent duty of any sovereign, both domestically and in relations with other sovereigns, is to protect its own citizens. To modern globalists, however, defending sovereignty is selfish – and even aggressive – behavior, which gives rise to a moral imperative to restrain such selfishness.

A mandatory global cap-and-trade regime would also undermine sovereignty by intruding in the relationship between sovereigns and their own citizens. It would change the way individuals operate their businesses, what kinds of light bulbs they buy, and what kinds of cars they drive. It would punish individuals when they fail to comply with the edicts of a global entity with power to protect the earth's atmosphere. In this critically important way, global environmental law – particularly a cap-and-trade system – is a far cry from the traditional understanding of the treaty power, whereby treaties governed commitments at the sovereign-to-sovereign level, not the sovereign-to-individual level. It illustrates how the ever-morphing, ever-expanding, ever-creeping nature of international law threatens to choke traditional sovereignty, allowing an international body – with no political accountability to individual citizens – to control those citizens' behavior. In the words of a UN report on Agenda 21, a UN blueprint for global environmental regulation that resulted from the 1992 UN Conference on Environment and Development,

"Effective execution of Agenda 21 [the global environmental agenda] will require a profound reorientation of all human society, unlike anything the world has ever experienced – a major shift in the priorities of both governments and individuals and an unprecedented redeployment of human and financial resources. This shift will demand that a concern for the environmental consequences of every human action be integrated into individual and collective decision-making at every level."

Global environmentalism is only the tip of an enormous internationalist iceberg. A never-ending array of treaties, protocols, conventions, and accords spews forth on a daily basis, and the United States faces tremendous pressure to join in each global hug. Even when the U.S. Senate rejects ratification through democratic deliberation, the globalists keep pushing the envelope, discovering new ways to implement their agenda. Consider, for example, the Law of the Sea Treaty (LOST), which defines and regulates the use of international waters, including such things as navigation, fishing, deep-seabed mining, and protection of the marine environment.

The United States hasn't signed or ratified LOST, believing that it isn't in the nation's best interests. One concern, for example, is that LOST establishes that parties to the treaty can't interfere with the ships of other nations while on the high seas. Although there are some exceptions to this general rule, none would allow parties to intercept ships operated by terrorists who might want to transport weapons or personnel using ships. In addition, U.S. naval intelligence and training missions could trigger mandatory jurisdiction by the International Tribunal for the Law of the Sea (ITLOS), a court centered in Hamburg, Germany. The tribunal has twenty-one judges representing states that have ratified the treaty, including states potentially hostile to U.S. interests, such as Brazil, Cameroon, China, Ghana, Lebanon, Senegal, Russia, and Tunisia. The tribunal can claim jurisdiction over any matter covered by the treaty, and its decisions cannot be appealed. Also, LOST is problematic because it allows taxes and license fees to be levied for party states' activities in the deep seabed. Such taxation on U.S. businesses – assessed and collected by an international entity, beyond the territorial borders of any other existing sovereign – would be unprecedented. The entity that collects these taxes, the International Seabed Authority, is given broad discretion to redistribute this wealth to party states according to "equitable sharing criteria, taking into account the interests and needs of developing States."

Consider also the case of the International Criminal Court (ICC), a court with jurisdiction to prosecute – without a jury trial – amorphous crimes such as genocide, crimes against humanity, war crimes, and crimes of aggression. President Bill Clinton signed the ICC treaty in 2000 but didn't submit it to the Senate for ratification, stating that he believed that the United States "should have the chance to observe and assess the functioning of the court, over time, before choosing to become subject to its jurisdiction." President George W. Bush's decision two years later to "unsign" the treaty sparked outrage among globalists.

Unsigning a treaty essentially means that the nation becomes completely unattached from its obligations and can take overt actions to undermine its object and purpose. It's perhaps with particular relish, therefore, that the globalists now actively seek to indict President Bush for war crimes in the jurisdiction of the ICC. Although the United States hasn't ratified the ICC treaty, the treaty's broad jurisdictional reach encompasses acts committed within the borders of more than one hundred nations that are a party to the treaty. Indeed, in January 2010, international law professor Francis Boyle of the University of Illinois College of Law filed a formal complaint with the ICC – as yet unresolved – against President Bush, Vice President Cheney, Secretary of Defense Donald Rumsfeld, Secretary of State Condoleezza Rice, CIA Director George Tenet, and U.S. Attorney General Alberto Gonzales, alleging that the practice of "extraordinary rendition" and subsequent torture of suspected al-Qaeda terrorists constitutes a crime against humanity.

The internationalist agenda to undermine U.S. sovereignty extends beyond formal UN treaties, conventions, protocols, and accords. There's a less obvious, but equally weighty, threat emanating from within – namely, judges' use of foreign or international law to interpret the U.S. Constitution. Here's how Harold Koh, the current legal adviser of the State Department and former international law professor at Yale, explained the situation:

> [T]he Supreme Court has now divided into transnationalist and nationalist factions, which hold sharply divergent attitudes toward transnational law.... The transnationalists believe in and promote the blending of international and domestic law; while nationalists continue to maintain a rigid separation of domestic from foreign law. The transnationalists view domestic courts as having a critical role to play in domesticating international law into U.S. law, while nationalists argue instead that only the political branches can internalize international law. The transnationalists believe the U.S.

courts can and should use their interpretive powers to promote the development of a global legal system, while the nationalists tend to claim that U.S. courts should limit their attention to the development of a national system.

The transnationalists (globalists) on the Court are progressives or liberals – Justices Breyer, Ginsburg, Kagan, and Sotomayor. The nationalists are conservatives – Alito, Scalia, Thomas, and Chief Justice Roberts. As usual, Justice Kennedy holds the balance of power as the swing vote on contentious issues, and his record on the use of international and foreign law in U.S. constitutional interpretation is not encouraging. Indeed, Justice Kennedy authored the Supreme Court's majority opinions in two cases that I'll use to illustrate the problems inherent in using international and foreign law to interpret the Constitution: (1) *Roper v. Simmons* and (2) *Lawrence v. Texas*. In both *Roper* and *Lawrence*, the Court ruled state laws unconstitutional, relying at least partially on the persuasive authority of foreign and international law.

In *Roper v. Simmons*, the Court was asked to decide whether state laws allowing the death penalty for sixteen- or seventeen-year-old juveniles accused of capital crimes violated the Eighth Amendment's prohibition of cruel and unusual punishment. Christopher Simmons was seven months shy of his eighteenth birthday when he and two of his younger friends (ages fifteen and sixteen) decided, in a cold, premeditated manner, to burglarize and murder someone. They picked the house of Shirley Crook, who was home alone. They abducted Crook, binding her hands and feet with electrical wire and wrapping her head in duct tape. They drove her to a nearby bridge and dropped her into the river below.

Simmons bragged to his friends that he murdered Crook because "the bitch seen my face." After informants tipped off the police, Simmons was arrested, waived his rights, and confessed to the murder after two hours of interrogation. The state of Missouri charged Simmons with murder in the first degree and sought the death penalty. A jury found Simmons guilty and, after hearing testimony regarding aggravating and mitigating factors, it recommended capital punishment.

At the time *Roper* was decided, thirty states had laws prohibiting the death penalty for all juveniles younger than eighteen. Twenty states – including Missouri – still allowed it for juveniles aged sixteen or seventeen, provided the jury considered all aggravating and mitigating factors, including the defendant's age. And only sixteen years before *Roper*, the Supreme Court had held, in *Stanford v. Kentucky* (1989), that capital punishment for sixteen- or seventeen-year-old murderers did not violate the Eighth Amendment.

Despite the recent precedent in *Stanford*, the Court in *Roper* held, by a narrow 5–4 margin, that executing Simmons would be cruel and unusual punishment in violation of the Eighth Amendment. In reaching its decision, the Court relied on various factors, including social science data indicating that juveniles are immature and irresponsible, the fact that execution of juveniles in the United States was rare, and – most important for present purposes – the "opinion of the world community."

Justice Kennedy's majority opinion noted that "the United States is the only country in the world that continues to give official sanction to the juvenile death penalty." The majority then cited the UN Convention on the Rights of the Child and the International Covenant on Civil and Political Rights, both of which prohibit the death penalty for individuals younger than age eighteen. The United States has refused to ratify the UN convention, and although it ratified the covenant, it insisted on a reservation that declares: "the United States reserves the right... to impose capital punishment on any person (other than a pregnant woman) duly convicted under existing or future laws permitting the imposition of capital punishment, including such punishment for crimes committed by persons below the age of eighteen years of age."

The fact that the United States had – through its constitutional, democratic process – rejected treaty obligations outlawing the juvenile death penalty proved irrelevant to the internationalists on the *Roper* Court. They concluded: "It is proper that we acknowledge the overwhelming weight of international opinion against the juvenile death penalty, resting in large part on the understanding that the instability and emotional imbalance of young people may often be a factor in the crime. The opinion of the world community, while not controlling our outcome, *does provide respected and significant confirmation of our own conclusions*" (emphasis added). The Court then tried to assuage concerns about using international law as a "respected and significant" confirmatory source of relevant interpretive data by saying, "It does not lessen our fidelity to the Constitution or our pride it its origins to acknowledge that the express affirmation of certain fundamental rights by other nations and peoples simply underscores the centrality of those same rights within our own heritage of freedom."

But how can it not "lessen our fidelity to the Constitution" to look to international and foreign laws for "respected and significant confirmation" of a specific interpretive outcome? Isn't it *our* Constitution the Justices are supposed to be interpreting, with due regard to what *Americans* think about the issue? As Justice Scalia pointed out in his *Roper* dissent, the majority used international and foreign law *"to set aside* the centuries-old American practice... of letting a jury of 12 citizens decide whether, in the particular case, youth should be the basis for withholding the death penalty. What these foreign sources 'affirm,' rather than repudiate, is the Justices' own notion of how the world ought to be, and their diktat that it shall be so henceforth in America.... 'Acknowledgement' of foreign approval has no place in the legal opinion of this Court *unless it is part of the basis for the Court's judgment* – which is surely what it parades as today" (emphasis in original).

From an originalist perspective – a perspective embraced by the Tea Party, as I discuss extensively in the following chapter – there's no doubt whatsoever that the founding generation thought the death penalty was constitutional, leaving the development of any restrictions on the practice solely up to future democratic legislative processes. The Due Process Clauses of the Fifth and Fourteenth Amendments make this abundantly clear, declaring that neither the federal nor state governments may deprive persons of "life, liberty, or property, without due process of law." Inherent in this declaration is the fact that governments may, in fact, deprive persons of life, so long as due process (e.g., a fair trial) is provided.

But even assuming that one rejects originalism in favor of the concept of a living Constitution, the salient question should be what attitudes, beliefs, and principles Americans held about the death penalty for sixteen- and seventeen-year-olds in 2005, when *Roper* was decided. On this issue, there was clearly an ongoing debate in the United States, and no clear consensus had emerged. This alone should have cautioned

the Supreme Court not to intervene and impose its own subjective policy preferences over those of democratically elected
state legislators.

The second case that illustrates the debate about international and foreign law in U.S. constitutional interpretation
is *Lawrence v. Texas* (2003). In *Lawrence*, a five-Justice majority invalidated a Texas statute that criminalized homosexual
sodomy, concluding that it violated the "liberty" component
of the Due Process Clause. In so concluding, the Court overruled binding precedent it had established just seventeen
years earlier, in *Bowers v. Hardwick* (1986).

In reversing *Bowers*, the *Lawrence* majority said the following: "To the extent *Bowers* relied on values we share
with a wider civilization, it should be noted that the reasoning and holding in *Bowers* have been rejected elsewhere.
The European Court of Human Rights has not followed
Bowers.... Other nations, too, have taken action consistent
with an affirmation of the protected right of homosexual adults
to engage in intimate, consensual conduct. The right petition-
ers seek in this case has been accepted as an integral part of
human freedom in many other countries. There has been no
showing that in this country the governmental interest in cir-
cumscribing personal choice is somehow more legitimate or
urgent."

Justice Kennedy's majority opinion in *Lawrence* is fascinating because it sets up a straw man – "To the extent *Bowers*
relied on values we share with a wider civilization" – and
then cuts it down, using international and foreign law as its
sickle. As Justice Scalia noted in his dissent, *Bowers* in fact
never made any reference to "values" of a "wider civilization" but "rather rejected the claimed right to sodomy on the
ground that such a right was not 'deeply rooted in *this Nation's*

history and tradition" (emphasis in original). This has historically been the Supreme Court's approach to liberty claims under the Due Process Clause: it asks whether the asserted liberty is something that has been "deeply rooted in this Nation's history and tradition," then proceeds to look at historical legal treatment of the issue, including colonial law and any deeper roots in English law.

Under this traditional approach to interpreting constitutional liberty claims, the foreign law that is examined to aid constitutional interpretation is limited to English law with direct historical linkage to subsequent colonial and state law. English law is considered relevant in this limited context because it sheds light on what those who wrote and ratified our own Constitution may have thought their language – in this case, the word *liberty* – meant. If something like sodomy isn't "deeply rooted in this Nation's history and tradition," the reasoning goes, it's reasonable to conclude that the word *liberty* in our Constitution wasn't meant to shelter it from reasonable legislative restrictions.

The use of foreign and international law in *Roper* and *Lawrence* also illustrates another inherent problem: Which foreign or international law counts? Should the Court make a tally sheet of every country and see which side of an issue has more support around the globe? Are some countries' laws – other than early English law that formed the basis of subsequent American law – more important to consider than others? Is Germany's law, for example, more influential than Brazil's or Pakistan's? And which is more persuasive, international law (that the United States by definition hasn't ratified) or the law of individual countries? Is a UN treaty that the United States has rejected more, or less, influential than the domestic law of South Africa?

As these few preliminary questions show, there's no principled way for U.S. judges to invoke foreign or international law when interpreting the Constitution. As Justice Scalia pointed out in *Roper*, if international and foreign law is relevant to U.S. constitutional interpretation, it should be consistently used in every case; otherwise, it's subjectivism run amok. In deciding to what extent the U.S. Constitution protects a woman's right to abortion, for example, the Supreme Court should presumably be influenced by the fact that only a handful of countries allow abortion past the first trimester and reverse its prior decisions allowing abortion until fetal viability. It should also matter that, in the context of interpreting the First Amendment's Establishment Clause – which has been interpreted to require a high degree of separation between church and state – most other countries don't require such rigid separation, allowing the government to fund religious schools and other endeavors. It would also seem imperative to interpret our Second Amendment – which gives us a right to keep and bear arms – in a manner consistent with the laws of other countries, the vast majority of which prohibit gun ownership.

The cold, hard, politically incorrect truth is that American judges shouldn't care what other countries think because their job is to interpret *our* Constitution. The only thing that is relevant is what the Constitution's words meant (or presently mean, if you are a living constitutionalist) to We the People. Our judges are required to take an oath under Article VI of the Constitution, which binds them "to support *this* Constitution" (emphasis added). And whether an individual judge likes it or not, our Constitution is, in many respects, unique. This should be a source of pride, not shame. We don't need to norm our Constitution with the rest of the world. We need to protect and defend it.

Indeed, let's step back and examine the larger picture in *Roper* and *Lawrence* to get some perspective on where they may lead. In both cases, the Supreme Court seemed to be going out of its way to cite foreign and international law. It's like the Court decided, at the very end of its analysis, to tack on some cool-sounding foreign and international law, as if to say, "Oh, and by the way, the wider international community agrees with the decision we've already made." This seems innocent enough – it's a form of bolstering rather than actual reliance – but one is left wondering, Why venture into such a controversial intellectual tar pit? If foreign and international law isn't really helping the Court interpret the Constitution, why cite it at all? Could there be any usefulness to doing it?

Innocently referencing foreign and international law in constitutional cases – using it as bolstering evidence – is the proverbial camel's nose in the tent. It's a first step, but certainly not the last, given the evolution inherent in common law adjudication. What's merely an interesting observation today becomes persuasive authority tomorrow and a basis for decision sometime after that.

The cumulative effect, year after year, of courts acknowledging international or foreign law in constitutional cases is establishing an analytical framework for implementing the globalist agenda in ways unachievable through the political branches. Federal judges are unelected and tenured for life. And although it's possible for federal judges to be impeached, impeachment is incredibly rare and, given the nature of what is occurring in cases like *Roper* and *Lawrence*, highly unlikely to occur. Citing foreign and international law sources as "interesting," "useful" or even "persuasive" isn't by itself unconstitutional. But as this sort of reasoning evolves and becomes more common, the potential for foreign and international norms to overtly or covertly alter the meaning of our Constitution is obvious. Convincing the federal judiciary to cite international and foreign law can morph into a means of undermining, and ultimately bypassing, American principles, values, and norms. If globalists want to remake the Constitution, convincing the federal judiciary to use foreign and international law is an effective and efficient strategy.

B. The War on Terror

Defending one's territory and citizenry is the very heart of sovereignty. Under the law of nations – the original form of international law, understood and embraced by the founders of our country – self-defense was acknowledged to be a natural right of sovereigns, just as it was for individuals. When the United States was attacked by al-Qaeda on September 11, 2001, it invoked the right to defend itself against further attacks by initiating the "war on terror." In the words of President Bush in his State of the Union address, just four months after 9/11: "Our nation will continue to be steadfast and patient and persistent in the pursuit of two great objectives: First, we will shut down terrorist camps, disrupt terrorist plans, and bring terrorists to justice. And, second, we must prevent the terrorists and regimes who seek chemical, biological or nuclear weapons from threatening the United States and the world."

On September 14, 2001 – only three days after 9/11 – President Bush sought and obtained authorization from

Congress to "use all necessary and appropriate force against those nations, organizations, or persons he determines planned, authorized, committed, or aided the terrorist attacks that occurred on September 11, 2001, or harbored such organizations or persons, in order to prevent any future acts of international terrorism against the United States by such nations, organizations or persons." Under this authorization, President Bush ordered the U.S. military to enter Afghanistan with the goal of striking al-Qaeda terrorist training camps and military installations of the supportive Taliban regime.

Compared to the military action in Afghanistan, the war in Iraq had a much more complex legal history. More than a year after 9/11 – toward the end of 2002 – President Bush, upon receipt of intelligence that Saddam Hussein was stockpiling weapons of mass destruction (WMDs), began urging the United Nations to enforce numerous prior resolutions mandating Iraqi disarmament. He addressed the UN General Assembly on September 12, 2002, outlining the case for UN action and requesting a "new [Security Council] resolution to meet our common challenge." One month later, in October 2002, the U.S. Congress overwhelmingly passed a second resolution authorizing the use of military force – this time, specifically addressing the developing situation in Iraq, and authorizing the president to use the military force "he determines to be necessary and appropriate in order to: (1) defend the national security of the United States against the continuing threat posed by Iraq; and (2) enforce all relevant United Nations Security Council resolutions against Iraq."

In response to the U.S. plea for action, in early November 2002 the Security Council unanimously approved Resolution 1441, which declared Iraq to be in "material breach" of prior resolutions requiring the destruction of WMDs and certain types of missiles and gave Iraq a "final opportunity" to comply. Resolution 1441 demanded a complete accounting of Iraqi weapons and "immediate, unimpeded, unconditional, and unrestricted access to any and all . . . areas, facilities, buildings, equipment, records, and means of transport" for UN weapons inspectors.

Iraq agreed to Resolution 1441 and inspectors entered Iraq. Chief UN weapons inspector Hans Blix reported to the Security Council in February 2003 that there were still unresolved "issues of anthrax, the nerve agent VX and long-range missiles" and that Iraq's report regarding its weaponry "missed the opportunity to provide the fresh material and evidence needed to respond to the open questions." Blix admitted that inspectors had discovered missiles capable of exceeding the range prohibited by prior UN resolutions and revealed that "a number of persons have declined to be interviewed" by UN inspectors. He further indicated that aircraft surveillance would soon begin to ascertain whether Iraq was moving weapons around by truck, based on "persistent intelligence reports . . . about mobile biological weapons production units." On March 7, 2003, Blix again addressed the Security Council, reporting that, as an aid in determining whether mobile weapons units existed, inspectors were hoping "soon to be able to add night vision capability" through a special Russian aircraft. He admitted that no mobile weapons units had "so far been found," nor had underground facilities for making or storing WMDs been "found so far." Blix concluded that Iraq had recently been more cooperative and that such measures were "welcome" and presented some "hope of solving presently unresolved disarmament issues."

Shortly after Blix's March report, the United States and Great Britain began circulating a draft Security Council resolution authorizing the use of military force against Iraq. But President Jacques Chirac of France – a permanent Security Council member – dashed hopes of UN support for military action when he told the press a few days later, "My position is that whatever the circumstances, France will vote no." When Russian Foreign Minister Igor Ivanov announced that Russia, too, would veto the U.S.-U.K. resolution, the Bush administration withdrew the draft and decided to move forward without UN backing. A few days later, on March 20, 2003, a coalition of twenty nations led by the United States and Great Britain commenced preemptive military action against Iraq. Within weeks, Baghdad had fallen, and Saddam Hussein had been captured.

Globalists uniformly condemned the United States for taking military action without the blessing of the UN Security Council. Kofi Annan, UN secretary-general, told the press in 2004 that U.S. military action in Iraq "was not in conformity with the U.N. charter. From our point of view and from the charter point of view it was illegal." A 551-page report issued by the Dutch government in January 2010 similarly concluded that the military action "had no sound mandate in international law." Numerous internationalist law professors have condemned U.S. military action in Iraq as "illegal," citing their belief that without the explicit blessing of the UN Security Council, preemptive military force can never, or virtually never, constitute self-defense.

The globalists' position is that the "lawful" use of military force requires either (1) the explicit blessing of the UN Security Council or (2) an "imminent" threat of attack. The first scenario – a prerequisite blessing by the Security Council – is simply ludicrous. There's nothing in existing treaties that requires nations to obtain the blessing of the

UN Security Council before taking unilateral military action. And even if it did, it wouldn't matter for one simple reason: a treaty cannot trump the U.S. Constitution.

Article II, section 2, of the Constitution declares that the president is the commander in chief of the armed forces. This declaration gives the president power to order the armed forces into military action whenever U.S. interests demand it. Although Congress has a separate power under Article I, section 8, to "declare war," this has never been understood – despite popular misunderstanding to the contrary – to require a formal declaration of war by Congress before the president engages U.S. military forces as commander in chief. Presidents have employed the U.S. military more than one hundred times since the Constitution was ratified, but there has been a formal declaration of war by Congress only five times: the War of 1812, the Mexican-American War, the Spanish-American War, World War I, and World War II.

This is not to say that the president's commitment of U.S. troops to a conflict is none of Congress's business. To the contrary: Congress has the power of the purse and can always cut off funding for military efforts undertaken by the president without a declaration of war. This was how the United States ended its involvement in Vietnam, for which no formal declaration of war was ever made. Moreover, the longer and more extensive the commitment of U.S. troops, the more a formal declaration of war becomes politically desirable, even if not constitutionally required. Congressional blessing of the president's commitment of troops adds political legitimacy, assuring that We the People support the president's action. This likely explains why President Bush sought and received congressional approval for two separate authorizations for the use of military force – the first before deploying troops in

Afghanistan, the second when deploying troops in Iraq. But whatever one's views on the degree or timing of congressional involvement desirable for U.S. troop commitment, one thing is clear: the Constitution doesn't require prior approval by the UN Security Council. The propriety of the use of U.S. military force is solely a question for the U.S. political branches – the president and Congress – to resolve.

The second globalist position – that military forces can be used without Security Council blessing only when there is an actual or imminent threat to the United States – is not supported by either the Constitution or pragmatism. The Constitution contains no language even remotely suggesting that the president as commander in chief can call U.S. forces into action only when a threat is imminent. This doesn't mean, however, that presidents won't use their political and common sense to use U.S. forces only when they deem it necessary for the protection of American interests. No sovereign can predict with 100 percent accuracy the nature and timing of a perceived threat. There are clearly some situations in which preemptive military force is in America's best interests, saving both blood and treasure. Do the internationalists believe that preemptive force is never legal? Surely not, for this would eviscerate the doctrine of self-defense, giving aggressors a free pass to strike. Indeed, this was exactly the threat posed by Iraq: the United States was attacked by terrorists affiliated with al-Qaeda. Iraq was a country with a history of supporting terrorist organizations. When U.S. intelligence revealed that the Iraqi regime was potentially pursuing a nuclear weapons program and stockpiling WMDs, it gave rise to a reasonable fear that Iraq would either use such weapons or share them with terrorists. Iraq eventually cried uncle and allowed in UN inspectors. But the UN inspectors' reports were at best inconclusive and incomplete, and the United States and its allies had no way of knowing for certain whether Iraq was six months or six days or six hours away from striking against the United States or its allies. Were the United States and its allies supposed to wait to be attacked by terrorists again? Many globalists say yes.

Other globalists take a more nuanced approach, suggesting that for the use of military force to be legitimate, a sovereign must be "reasonably certain" that an attack is imminent. But what does this mean? Is a 75 percent degree of certainty sufficient, or 50 percent? How can anyone know, without the benefit of hindsight, what degree of certainty exists regarding the imminence of any particular threat? Moreover, is the imminence requirement satisfied if the attack is anticipated within a week? A month? Six months?

Every sovereign must make its own informed decision about what degree of risk it deems acceptable when the lives of its own citizen are potentially on the line. No global entity can or should second-guess this decision – doing so is an extremely dangerous form of Monday-morning quarterbacking, perverted further by a high potential for politicization. Americans shouldn't tolerate globalists who want to handcuff our elected leaders from making their best judgments regarding our safety. Defending the safety of U.S. citizens is a non-delegable duty that belongs to our president and Congress.

The Obama administration shares the globalists' view that U.S. military force can be "legally" used only when either (1) the UN Security Council has concurred or (2) there is an imminent threat to the United States. This likely explains why President Obama recently committed U.S. armed forces to combat operations in Libya when – unlike the situation in Iraq – there was no evidence that Libya was stockpiling chemical or biological weapons or pursuing a nuclear program. In President Obama's televised address to the American people, he explained why he'd authorized the use of troops: "Qaddafi declared he would show 'no mercy' to his own people. He compared them to rats, and threatened to go door to door to inflict punishment.... We knew that if we waited – if we waited one more day, Benghazi, a city nearly the size of Charlotte, could suffer a massacre that would have reverberated across the region and stained the conscience of the world. It was not in our national interest to that let happen. I refused to let that happen.... I authorized military action to stop the killing and enforce U.N. Security Council Resolution 1973." Security Council Resolution 1973 was passed by a vote of 10–0, with five members abstaining (Brazil, China, Germany, India, and Russia). It condemned Qaddafi's violation of human rights; demanded an immediate cease-fire against rebels; and authorized member states "to take all necessary measures ... to protect civilians and civilian populated areas," including the establishment of a no-fly zone around designated areas of rebellion.

President Obama has faced intense criticism from both the political left and the right for his decision to commit troops in Libya. Both Republicans and Democrats in Congress have criticized the president's failure to obtain authorization from Congress – as President Bush had done – before committing U.S. troops abroad, particularly because there didn't appear to be an imminent threat to the United States. For example, Democratic Congressman Dennis Kucinich of Ohio declared in a press interview: "President Obama moved forward without Congress approving. He didn't have Congressional authorization, he has gone against the Constitution, and that's got to be said.... It would appear on its face to be an impeachable offense." Others, mostly conservative Republicans, have criticized the president's act of seeking Security Council authorization before committing troops. The concern is that seeking prior international approval – particularly when congressional approval isn't obtained – implicitly endorses the idea that the president lacks sovereign power to unilaterally deploy U.S. military forces. In the words of the conservative *Washington Times* editorial board, "By bowing to the will of the U.N. Security Council, President Obama is diluting the sovereign power of the United States."

From the perspective of protecting U.S. sovereignty, President Obama's insistence on obtaining Security Council approval before using U.S. military force is troubling. Under the U.S. Constitution, the question of whether to commit U.S. troops is no other nation's business but our own. The president has authority as commander in chief; Congress has authority to declare war and control the purse strings if it disagrees with any decision of the president. It may be nice bolstering to obtain UN approval before using U.S. military force abroad, but it's certainly not necessary. This may explain why President Bush and British Prime Minister Tony Blair tried, albeit unsuccessfully, to obtain Security Council approval before initiating military action in Iraq.

There's a fine line, however, between obtaining UN approval as extra insurance that bolsters the legitimacy of U.S. military action versus obtaining UN approval because one thinks it's legally necessary. In this sense, President Obama's decision to go to the Security Council and not the U.S. Congress for approval is disturbing for the same reason as the Supreme Court's recent citation of foreign and international law to aid U.S. constitutional interpretation. In both instances, we have a branch of the U.S. government – the president in one case, the federal judiciary in another – that is sending signals that U.S. constitutional law is no longer the sole province of Americans. If our Supreme Court needs to canvass foreign and international law before interpreting the U.S. Constitution – if it can't interpret the Constitution solely by referencing *American* principles and values – then American sovereignty to interpret its own charter of government has been diminished. If our president needs UN approval before committing U.S. troops – if he can't do it whenever he believes it to be in America's best interest – then he's lost sovereignty (power) as commander in chief. Americans – particularly Tea Partiers – would think it odd that either our Supreme Court or our president would think they need to consult with the international community before doing what they think is right for America.

The Obama administration's globalist approach to national security is also evident in its odd reticence to criticize Islamic terrorism or to even utter the words *Islamists, Islamic jihad,* or *terrorism*. Such political correctness is the direct result of an internationalist culture that threatens U.S. sovereignty. Consider the remarks of John Brennan, President Obama's deputy national security adviser for homeland security and counterterrorism, who declared in classic internationalist style:

> Values – respect for universal values, at home and around the world defines who we are and what we hold dear. And an international order that promotes peace, security, and opportunity through stronger cooperation as this the only path that will allow us to meet global challenges.... The President's strategy is absolutely clear about the threat we face. Our enemy is not "terrorism"

because terrorism is but a tactic. Our enemy is not "terror" because terror is a state of mind and as Americans we refuse to live in fear. Nor do we describe our enemy as "jihadists" or "Islamists" because jihad is a holy struggle, a legitimate tenant of Islam, meaning to purify oneself or one's community, and there is nothing holy or legitimate or Islamic about murdering innocent men, women and children.

Notice that Brennan begins by appealing to "universal values," not American values. And he assumes an "international order" is the "only path" for meeting "global challenges." The vision articulated is one of integrating the United States more deeply into an international order and forcing the United States to act collectively, not individualistically. This vision will eviscerate U.S. sovereignty.

As we've seen with the European Union, multilateral institutions aren't democratic institutions. They aren't accountable to We the People and cannot be expected to respond to our preferences or honor our Constitution. Multilateral institutions are monolithic bureaucracies that cater to the least common denominator. If you think getting Washington, D.C., to listen to your needs is difficult, it would be a hundred times worse if you had to appeal to some multilateral bureaucracy in Brussels.

Brennan's statement also revealed the Obama administration's allegiance to globalist political correctness. We shouldn't call it terrorism because that might offend Muslims. Instead, let's call it, as Homeland Security Secretary Janet Napolitano insists, a "man-caused disaster." And let's not refer to jihadists, Islamists, or even radical Islam because that might offend Muslims, too. One need look no further than the Fort Hood shooting of November 2009 to see this demented worldview in full bloom. Army Major Nidal Malik Hasan, a Palestinian American, opened fire on the Texas Army base, shouting "Allahu akbar!" ("God is great!" in Arabic), killing thirteen people and wounding more than thirty others. Hasan, a psychiatrist, had ties to a radical imam named Anwar al-Aulaqi, who had counseled two of the 9/11 attackers months before their attack and praised Hasan as a hero after the shootings.

The Obama administration has refused to label Hasan's act as an act of terrorism. In an interview on ABC's *This Week*, Army Chief of Staff General George Casey assiduously avoided labeling Hasan as a terrorist, stating that calling it terrorism "could potentially heighten backlash against some of our Muslim soldiers" and concluding that "what happened at Fort Hood was a tragedy, but I believe it would be an even greater tragedy if our diversity becomes a casualty here." A *New York Times* article on November 6, 2009, painted a sympathetic picture of Hasan as a loyal American who volunteered for the army because he loved his country. It even had the chutzpah to suggest that Hassan's acts were attributable to the fact that "soldiers harassed him for being a Muslim" and that he was "mortified by the idea of having to deploy [to Afghanistan]."

Two additional *New York Times* articles on November 8, 2009, elaborated on this theme. One was titled "Painful Stories Take a Toll on Military Therapists" and asserted that military psychiatrists such as Hasan are bombarded with "repeated stories of battle and loss [that] can leave the most professional therapists numb or angry." It stated that such therapists have "crushing schedules" that cause "[s]ome to go home at night too depressed to talk to their children."

The other article, titled "Little Evidence of Terror Plot in Base Killings," reported that investigators had tentatively concluded that Hasan "acted out under a welter of emotional, ideological and religious pressures" and was not a terrorist because, although he logged onto radical jihadist Web sites, exchanged e-mails with radical Islamists, and posted comments to Web sites in support of Palestinian suicide bombers, there was "no evidence that Major Hasan sent e-mail messages to known terrorists or anyone else who encouraged or helped him to orchestrate the shootings." As former U.S. Attorney General Michael Mukasey observed in a speech to military families in Pennsylvania shortly after the shooting, "To tell us to believe that someone has to have a membership card in al-Qaeda or any other organization in order for them to act as a terrorist, and in order for us to call what he does an act of terrorism, is to tell us to refuse to look at facts in the face, and to refuse to believe what we see and hear with our own eyes and ears."

Under the progressive, politically correct view of the Fort Hood shooting, Hasan was a stressed-out victim, not a terrorist. He deserved our sympathy, not our condemnation. Maybe the military was to blame for overworking him or planning to deploy him. Maybe other soldiers were to blame for harassing him. Indeed, any suggestion that Hasan was a terrorist was portrayed as unreasonable, aggressive behavior that could trigger acts of violence against other Muslim Americans. But understandably concerned Americans knew better: a Rasmussen poll taken shortly after the shootings revealed that 60 percent wanted it to be "investigated by military authorities as a terrorist act." Hasan is currently being prosecuted by military authorities for criminal charges of murder and attempted murder.

The Obama administration's reticence to use the *t* word goes well beyond the Fort Hood shootings. Consider the contortions Attorney General Eric Holder had to undertake in his colloquy with Representative Lamar Smith during a May 2009 House Judiciary Committee hearing investigating domestic terrorist acts:

SMITH: Let me go to my next question, which is – in – in the case of all three attempts in the last year, the terrorist attempts, one of which was successful, those individuals have had ties to radical Islam. Do you feel that these individuals might have been incited to take the actions that they did because of radical Islam?

HOLDER: Because of?

SMITH: Radical Islam.

HOLDER: There are a variety of reasons why I think people have taken these actions. It's – one, I think you have to look at each individual case. I mean, we are in the process now of talking to Mr. Shahzad to try to understand what it is that drove him to take the action.

SMITH: Yes, but radical Islam could have been one of the reasons?

HOLDER: There are a variety of reasons why people...

SMITH: But was radical Islam one of them?

HOLDER: There are a variety of reasons why people do things. Some of them are potentially religious...

SMITH: OK. But all I'm asking is if you think among those variety of reasons radical Islam might have been one of the reasons that the individuals took the steps that they did.

HOLDER: You see, you say radical Islam. I mean, I think those people who espouse a – a version of Islam that is not...

SMITH: Are you uncomfortable attributing any other actions to radical Islam? It sounds like it.

HOLDER: No, I don't want to say anything negative about a religion that is not...

SMITH: No, no. I'm not talking about religion. I'm talking about radical Islam. I'm not talking about the general religion.

HOLDER: Right. And I'm saying that a person, like Anwar Awlaki, for instance, who has a version of Islam that is not consistent with the teachings of it...

SMITH: But...

HOLDER: ... and who espouses a radical version...

SMITH: But then is – could radical Islam had motivated these individuals to take the steps that they did?

HOLDER: I certainly think that it's possible that people who espouse a radical version of Islam have had an ability to have an impact on people like Mr. Shahzad.

SMITH: OK. And could it have been the case in one of these three instances?

HOLDER: Could that have been the case?

SMITH: Yes, could – again, could one of these three individuals have been incited by radical Islam? Apparently, you feel that that they could've been.

HOLDER: Well, I think potentially incited by people who have a view of Islam that is inconsistent with...

SMITH: OK. Mr. AG, it's hard to get an answer yes or no, but let me go on to my next question.

If the highest law enforcement officials in the United States aren't willing to use words that accurately describe the threat facing America, how safe can we be? If the present administration cannot even accept the fact that terrorism exists and is being planned and perpetrated by radical elements of Islam, should the American people have any confidence that it can protect us from such supposedly nonexistent phenomena? As Dorothy Rabinowitz recently concluded in a *Wall Street Journal* op-ed, "A country governed by leaders too principled to speak the name of its mortal enemy needs every infusion of reality it can get."

Globalist political correctness may also help explain the administration's initial decision to try 9/11 mastermind Khalid Sheikh Mohammed (KSM) and his coconspirators in a federal civilian court in New York rather than military tribunals. This decision was finally reversed in April 2011, concluding – as common sense should have dictated all along – that KSM will be tried by a military commission.

The Supreme Court has repeatedly ruled that it's constitutional to try unlawful enemy combatants – those who commit acts of aggression against the United States but don't wear an identifiable uniform or insignia, such as terrorists or spies – before a military commission. Unlawful enemy combatants are particularly dangerous enemies because, by definition, they're hard to spot: they move around in plain clothes, mixing with the general population. Their inherent surreptitiousness allows them to hide, posing a greater threat than lawful enemy combatants, who by definition are soldiers wearing identifiable uniforms and behaving by international rules of lawful engagement. In the words of the Supreme Court in *Ex Parte Quirin* (1942):

> Lawful combatants are subject to capture and detention as prisoners of war by opposing military forces. Unlawful combatants are likewise subject to capture and detention, but in addition they are subject to trial and

punishment by military tribunals for acts which render their belligerency unlawful. The spy who secretly and without uniform passes the military lines of a belligerent in time of war, seeking to gather military information and communicate it to the enemy, or an enemy combatant who without uniform comes secretly through the lines for the purpose of waging war by destruction of life or property, are familiar examples of belligerents who are generally deemed not to be entitled to the status of prisoners of war, but to be offenders against the law of war subject to trial and punishment by military tribunals.

Both lawful and unlawful enemy combatants can lawfully be detained indefinitely, until the duration of hostilities is over. This makes perfect sense, because if hostilities are still ongoing, releasing enemy combatants would allow them to threaten the United States all over again. This means that no trial of any sort is ever required for enemy combatants. We can keep them locked up until the war has ended.

After announcing in January 2009 that the terrorist detention facility at Guantánamo Bay, Cuba ("Gitmo"), would be "as soon as practicable, and no later than one year from the date of this [executive] order," the Obama administration finally admitted in March 2011 that it would – like the Bush administration before it – indefinitely detain some prisoners at Gitmo. Although this is a prudent and legally permissible course, the Obama administration's simultaneous decision to "choose out of a sense of legal obligation" to honor the requirements of Article 75 of Additional Protocol I of the 1949 Geneva Conventions is disturbing.

Article 75 would grant to unlawful enemy combatants – terrorists – the legal right to be treated the same as lawful enemy combatants (prisoners of war). It would prohibit, for example, any "violence" to the "mental well-being" or "outrages upon personal dignity" – or threats thereof – inflicted on a detained terrorist. Although these may sound laudable in the abstract, they would significantly hamper the collection of military intelligence from captured terrorists. For this reason, President Reagan informed the U.S. Senate in January 1987 that he would not submit Protocol I – containing Article 75, among other things – to the Senate for ratification. Though recognizing that some portions of Protocol I were meritorious, President Reagan concluded that "grant[ing] combatant status to irregular forces [i.e., unlawful enemy combatants] . . . would endanger civilians among whom terrorists and other irregulars attempt to conceal themselves." He explained that "we must not, and need not, give recognition and protection to terrorist groups as a price for progress in humanitarian law" and that rejecting Protocol I was "one additional step, at the ideological level so important to terrorist organizations, to deny these groups legitimacy as international actors."

The Obama administration's unilateral decision to "choose out of a sense of legal obligation" to accept Article 75 thus gives terrorists the very "legitimacy as international actors" that President Reagan so wisely refused to give them. By executive fiat – in nothing short of a dictatorial manner – President Obama has disrespected the role of the U.S. Senate in ratifying treaties, bypassing political input from We the People. Although President Obama may not agree with President Reagan that treating terrorists the same as prisoners of war would "endanger civilians," many Americans (and U.S. senators) presumably would, because eliminating the distinction of unlawful versus lawful enemy combatant for detention purposes creates a powerful legal disincentive to ever don uniforms and fight in the open. If you're going to wage war against another nation, why not take off those uniforms, hide among the civilian population, and behave like terrorists? Terrorists are more dangerous and effective precisely because they have the element of stealth. The Obama administration's unilateral decision to treat captured terrorists no differently than captured uniformed soldiers makes the world a more dangerous place and grants terrorists a degree of legal legitimacy they've never enjoyed before – at least not in the United States.

In bypassing U.S. Senate ratification of a controversial provision of a treaty, President Obama has, once again, given away a small but important slice of American sovereignty. He has placated the globalists who think the United States is "arrogant" when it fails to ratify every piece of paper spewed forth by the United Nations. As President Reagan understood in refusing to submit Protocol I to the Senate, "we cannot allow other nations of the world, however numerous, to impose upon us and our allies and friends an unacceptable and thoroughly distasteful price for joining a convention drawn to advance the laws of war." The politicization of international law to accommodate and legitimize terrorist activities isn't something the United States should support or condone. The president of the United States should do what's right for our country and its people, not cave in to peer pressure from globalists whose agenda is inherently antithetical to our own safety and sovereignty.

A globalist version of political correctness undergirds the administration's very public pronouncement to try terrorists such as KSM in ordinary courts rather than military commissions. Because it's clear from Supreme Court precedent and history that we don't have to try terrorists in ordinary courts, why would we? There are good reasons why military commissions have been established and, concomitantly, why trying terrorists in ordinary courts is a horrible idea. First is a simple matter of proving the circumstances of capture. Most terrorists are captured overseas during military or intelligence operations. For example, KSM was captured in Pakistan by a joint intelligence operation conducted by Pakistani and American forces. The soldiers or other officials who apprehend terrorists are sometimes difficult to ascertain or even know with certainty. In an ordinary criminal trial, the circumstances surrounding a criminal defendant's apprehension is relevant, and evidence relating to the apprehension must generally be proved through live testimony of the arresting officer. In the context capturing terrorists overseas, satisfying this evidentiary rule is often impossible. Military commissions, recognizing the difficulty of calling the soldier or other individual who apprehended the terrorist as a witness, allow such evidence to be proved by reliable affidavits instead.

Second, in an ordinary criminal court, the prosecutor is required to offer certain proof and turn potentially exculpatory evidence over to the accused, all of which could compromise national security by enabling terrorists to see sensitive information. For example, in an ordinary criminal trial involving a charge of conspiracy – such as the trial of KSM and his coconspirators – prosecutors must disclose the identity of all known coconspirators, even those who aren't prosecuted. Such disclosure tips off other suspected terrorists that they're being watched. Military tribunals, by contrast, restrict the accused's access to sensitive intelligence information.

Third, evidence obtained as a result of coercion is excluded in ordinary criminal trials. Terror suspects who were subjected to enhanced interrogation techniques such as waterboarding; stress positions; prolonged questioning; light, sound, or temperature manipulation; or even yelling could conceivably convince a judge to exclude any evidence obtained after using such interrogation techniques. Indeed, this happened in the trial of Ahmed Khalfan Ghailani, an al-Qaeda explosives expert who was captured and detained in Pakistan for his role in bombing U.S. embassies in Kenya and Tanzania. Ghailani was charged with more than 280 counts of murder and other offenses, but a jury convicted him of only one charge relating to his role in conspiring to bomb the buildings. Although Ghailani was sentenced to life in prison, his prosecution in the ordinary court cannot be characterized as successful. The jury's acquittal of Ghailani on all murder-related counts was likely caused by exclusion of the government's key witness, Hussein Abebe. The government learned about Abebe's identity from Ghailani after subjecting Ghailani to enhanced interrogation techniques. In the judge's view, these techniques rendered Abebe's testimony the fruit of a poisonous tree, requiring exclusion of all duress-related evidence. Specifically, the judge concluded that admitting such evidence would violate Ghailani's Fifth Amendment right not to be "compelled in any criminal case to be a witness against himself."

The judge's interpretation of the Fifth Amendment's Self-Incrimination Clause was novel, unsupported by prior Supreme Court decisions. The one appeals court case cited by the Ghailani trial judge that addressed the Fifth Amendment's Self-Incrimination Clause, *United States v. Sweets* (4th Cir., 2007), rejected the defendant's self-incrimination claim because revealing the identity of a person is not itself a self-incriminating fact: "Whether a statement or act, the testimonial communication 'must itself, explicitly or implicitly, relate a factual assertion or disclose information' that incriminates. This requirement removes from the Fifth Amendment's protection a myriad of compelled acts that, while leading to the discovery of incriminating evidence, do not themselves make an incriminating factual assertion." The judge in Ghailani's case dismissed *Sweets* cursorily, asserting, "[T]his Court does not agree with *Sweet's* view of the scope of the protection afforded by the Fifth Amendment right against self-incrimination. *Sweets* is not binding on this Court. To whatever extent that case might be regarded as inconsistent with the analysis and result reached here, this Court is unpersuaded by it." The same novel interpretation of the Self-Incrimination Clause would not likely be adopted by a military tribunal.

Equally important, the Ghailani case illustrates how unpredictable trying terrorists in ordinary courts can be, for the simple reason that terrorism cases aren't "normal" criminal cases. The way terrorists are apprehended, the way they're interrogated, and the way they're detained are very different from ordinary criminals. Unlawful enemy combatants aren't the same as the muggers and murderers who harm our neighbors; by definition, they're enemies of the country as a whole. The stakes are consequently much higher. As the Ghailani trial shows, ordinary courts aren't built for nonordinary terrorism cases, and many terrorism cases would risk similar unpredictable outcomes, which is probably why Attorney General Eric Holder reversed his decision to try KSM and his coconspirators in an ordinary court. Risking the acquittal of the self-proclaimed mastermind of 9/11 understandably wasn't an attractive option.

A fourth reason ordinary courts aren't a good idea is that the public nature of an ordinary criminal trial creates security risks not present with a nonpublic military tribunal proceeding. In the course of questioning witnesses, evidence can be elicited that could compromise U.S. intelligence. And the prospect of terror trials conducted in public courthouses would be a tempting target for radicals of all stripes, necessitating significantly heightened security procedures to protect the courthouses, judges, and jurors.

And finally, as constitutional lawyers David Rivkin and Lee Casey pointed out in a *Washington Examiner* op-ed in November 2009, trying terrorists as ordinary criminals "undermin[es] the legal architecture supporting the use of military force against al Qaeda." This is so because if terrorists "are not enemy combatants but civilian criminal suspects, then armed attacks by American soldiers against them are illegal." Soldiers who shoot at criminals, in other words, aren't really soldiers at all – they're police. And police can't use deadly force the way soldiers can. Soldiers can generally shoot first and ask questions later. Police can't do this – they have to attempt an arrest and, if the suspect tries to flee, they may or may not be able to use deadly force, depending on the circumstances. The bottom line, as Rivkin and Casey correctly conclude, is that trying terrorists as ordinary criminals "suggests that even the United States does not believe that it is engaged in a legally cognizable armed conflict but rather in a widespread law enforcement initiative," exposing U.S. service members to criminal liability for their use of force.

Not all terrorism cases, however, risk exposing the U.S. military to criminal liability. This is why trying terrorists such as Zacarias Moussaoui (the Twentieth Hijacker), Jose Padilla (the Dirty Bomber), and Umar Farouk Abdulmutallab (the Underwear Bomber) in ordinary courts was possible. They were all originally arrested on U.S. soil by ordinary law enforcement officers, not soldiers. So their trial as ordinary criminals didn't imply anything about the lawfulness of actions by American military personnel. By contrast, KSM and his coconspirators were captured overseas by military officials and should have immediately been understood as falling within the proper ambit of military legal process.

The Obama administration's decisions to adopt globalist positions in connection with the war on terror – closing Gitmo, trying terrorists in ordinary courts, unilaterally adopting Article 75, obtaining UN but not congressional approval before sending military forces into Libya, refusing to utter the *t* word – have had a cumulative negative impact on American sovereignty. If one listens carefully, one can almost hear the drip-drip-drip of U.S. sovereignty leaking away on national security issues. Little wonder, then, that an April 2011 Rasmussen poll revealed that only 32 percent of Americans think the U.S. and its allies are winning the war on terror – the lowest level since October 2006. If continued unchecked, the steady implementation of the globalist agenda relating to national security and the war on terror will irreparably weaken U.S. sovereignty and endanger U.S. interests.

C. Immigration

Although the war on terror illustrates the external aspect of sovereignty, the issue of illegal immigration exemplifies its internal aspect. Sovereigns must protect their citizens not only against attacks but also against erosion of their territorial integrity. Without the power to protect its own borders, a sovereign wouldn't be a sovereign for very long.

One of the most contentious immigration issues of the recent past – and one of great concern to the Tea Party – is how to deal with illegal immigration. According to a study published by the Pew Hispanic Center in February 2011, there are presently more than 11 million illegal immigrants living in the U.S. Illegal immigrants now constitute almost 4 percent of the U.S. population, more than 5 percent of the labor force, and 28 percent of the foreign-born population in the United States. The number of illegal immigrants living in the United States has tripled since 1990 and grown by more than a third since 2000. Americans' desire to defend their sovereign borders and stem the tide of illegal immigration can be illustrated by two recent issues: so-called birthright citizenship and the Arizona immigration law.

1. *Birthright Citizenship*

According to the Pew Hispanic Center, approximately 350,000 children are born in the United States to illegal immigrants each year. Under the Supreme Court's interpretation of the so-called Citizenship Clause of the Constitution, these children are instantly considered U.S. citizens by virtue of their birth on American soil. When these children reach the age of twenty-one, they are permitted by U.S. law to sponsor their parents and any siblings for U.S. citizenship – this is why they are often referred to as anchor babies. Until they reach that age, however, the anchor babies' parents (but not the anchor babies themselves) are subject to possible deportation.

Interestingly, the U.S. approach is unique. Few countries around the world permit birthright citizenship. The last EU country to do so was Ireland, which eliminated birthright citizenship in 2004, after a referendum overwhelmingly – by almost 80 percent – approved ending birthright citizenship for babies born in Ireland. The initiative was driven by a perceived need to stem the practice of citizenship tourism, whereby pregnant foreign women traveled to Ireland intending to give birth so their children could obtain an EU passport. Despite overwhelming opposition to birthright citizenship by other countries, progressives in the United States don't seem interested in following this particular global trend. Although other countries recognize the centrality of immigration to preserving their sovereignty, progressives in the United States are more worried about not offending immigrants.

The Citizenship Clause appears in section 1 of the Fourteenth Amendment to the Constitution and reads as follows: "All persons born or naturalized in the United States, and subject to the jurisdiction thereof, are citizens of the United States and of the State wherein they reside." The principal purpose of the Citizenship Clause was to reverse the Supreme Court's pre–Civil War decision in *Dred Scott v. Sandford* (1857), which concluded that no blacks of African descent – whether slave or free – could be considered a citizen of the United States. After the Civil War, in 1868, the Fourteenth Amendment was ratified. After ratification of the Fourteenth Amendment, therefore, no one could doubt that any black person born in the United States was a U.S. citizen.

But of course the text of the Fourteenth Amendment's Citizenship Clause wasn't limited to blacks – it refers to "all persons" born in the United States. And the historical record indicates that one of the primary purposes of proposing the Fourteenth Amendment was to provide a solid constitutional basis for upholding the broader Civil Rights Act of 1866, which among other things declared, "All persons born in the United States *and not subject to any foreign power, excluding Indians not taxed*, are hereby declared to be citizens of the United States" (emphasis added).

The Fourteenth Amendment's Citizenship Clause bears strong resemblance to the citizenship clause of the Civil Rights Act of 1866, although the two are not identical. The Constitution restricts birthright citizenship to individuals born in the United States and "subject to the jurisdiction thereof," whereas the Civil Rights Act restricts citizenship to those born in the United States "and not subject to any foreign power." The statute also specifically excludes Indians, whereas the constitutional text does not. The $6 million question for purposes of constitutional interpretation, therefore, is what does "subject to the jurisdiction thereof" mean? Did the framers and ratifiers of the Fourteenth Amendment think it meant the same thing as "not subject to any foreign power," or did it mean something entirely different?

The difference in phraseology between the Civil Rights Act of 1866 and the Fourteenth Amendment is potentially quite meaningful. Immigrants who enter the United States illegally are clearly "subject to [a] foreign power," and under the plain meaning of the Civil Rights Act of 1866, they are not entitled to automatic birthright citizenship. But the Fourteenth Amendment uses vaguer language – "subject to the jurisdiction thereof." Was this meant to convey only that the birth had to take place within the geographic territory of the United States? This seems highly unlikely, because it would make the amendment's preceding reference to those "born...in the United States" superfluous.

One important clue may be to consider the treatment of Indians. The Civil Rights Act of 1866 explicitly excludes "Indians not taxed" from birthright citizenship. The Fourteenth Amendment dropped this language and is entirely silent on the subject of the citizenship status of Indians. Did this imply that the framers and ratifiers of the Fourteenth Amendment meant to grant birthright citizenship to the Indians?

The answer is no. The Supreme Court in *Elk v. Wilkins* (1884) considered whether a native-born Indian who renounced his allegiance to his tribe could be considered "subject to the jurisdiction of the United States" within the meaning of the Citizenship Clause. The Court concluded that Indians were not entitled to birthright citizenship, reasoning that being "subject to the jurisdiction" of the U.S. required mutual consent – by the individual seeking U.S. citizenship as well as by the United States. The Court declared that the meaning of "subject to the jurisdiction of the United States" was "not merely subject in some respect or degree to the jurisdiction of the United States, but completely subject to their political jurisdiction and owing them direct and immediate allegiance.... Persons not thus subject to the jurisdiction of the United States at the time of birth cannot become so afterwards except by being naturalized."

Under the interpretation of the Citizenship Clause in *Wilkins*, babies born to illegal immigrants are not entitled to automatic U.S. citizenship under the Constitution, although they may be entitled to citizenship via naturalization statutes enacted by Congress. Under *Wilkins*, therefore, Indians and children born to illegal immigrants are given the same status. This would mean that, under Congress's Article I, section 8 power to "establish a uniform rule of naturalization," both Indians and illegal immigrants' babies born in the United States could possibly become citizens if Congress permitted it. Indeed, with regard to native-born Indians, Congress has done this.

The Court's decision in *Elk v. Wilkins*, however, did not specifically address babies of illegal immigrants because the case technically involved only the birthright citizenship of Indians. As such, its language about children born to foreigners was only dicta, subject to clarification and change in subsequent case law. In deciding this question, the courts might choose to consider what meaning the Citizenship Clause had to the members of Congress who wrote and voted on the measure. For example, Senator Jacob Howard of Michigan – the chief sponsor of the Fourteenth Amendment in the Senate – told his colleagues in the Senate that the Citizenship Clause he authored would "not, of course, include persons born in the United States who are foreigners, aliens, who belong to the families of ambassadors or foreign ministers accredited to the Government of the United States, but will include every other class of persons." Similarly, Senator Lyman Trumbull of Illinois, chair of the Senate Judiciary Committee, declared, "What do we [the Judiciary Committee] mean by 'subject to the jurisdiction of the United States'? Not owing allegiance to anyone else. That is what it means."

These statements by prominent members of Congress suggest that "subject to the jurisdiction of the United States" was meant to refer to allegiance to the country. Because Indians didn't owe allegiance to the United States, they, too, would be excluded from the Citizenship Clause's ambit, consistent with *Elk v. Wilkins*. But it wouldn't merely be Indians who were excluded under this interpretation – any foreigner who owed allegiance to another country would be excluded as well. And because children born in the United States of foreign parents could not be properly said to have any allegiance to the United States, arguably they would be excluded as well.

The birthright citizenship status of immigrants' children was finally settled by the Supreme Court's decision in *United States v. Wong Kim Ark* (1898), in which a young man born in the United States to Chinese parents left the country at age twenty-one to visit China. On his return to the United States, Wong Kim Ark was denied reentry on grounds that he was not a U.S. citizen. The Supreme Court phrased the constitutional question this way: "The question presented by the record is whether a child born in the United States, of parents of Chinese descent, who, at the time of his birth, are subjects of the Emperor of China, but have a permanent domicil [*sic*] and residence in the United States, and are there carrying on business, and are not employed in any diplomatic or official capacity under the Emperor of China, becomes at the time of his birth a citizen of the United States by virtue of the first clause of the Fourteenth Amendment of the Constitution." The Court answered this question in the affirmative, concluding that the Citizenship Clause

> affirms the ancient and fundamental rule of citizenship by birth within the territory, in the allegiance and under the protection of the country, including all children here born of resident aliens, with the exceptions or quali-fications (as old as the rule itself) of children of for-eign sovereigns or their ministers, or born on foreign public ships, or of enemies within and during a hos-tile occupation of part of our territory, and with the single additional exception of children of members of the Indian tribes owing direct allegiance to their several tribes.... Every citizen or subject of another country,

while domiciled here, is within the allegiance and the protection, and consequently subject to the jurisdiction, of the United States. To hold that the Fourteenth Amendment of the Constitution excludes from citizenship the children, born in the United States, of citizens or subjects of other countries would be to deny citizenship to thousands of persons of English, Scotch, Irish, German, or other European parentage who have always been considered and treated as citizens of the United States.

Technically, the holding of *Wong Kim Ark* addresses only the children born to immigrants residing legally in the United States at the time of the child's birth. Wong Kim Ark's Chinese parents were described by the Court as "subjects of the Emperor of China, but [with] a permanent domicil [*sic*] and residence in the United States." But *Wong Kim Ark*'s language is sufficiently broad to extend birthright citizenship to children born of illegal immigrants as well, and this has in fact been the way the case has been applied. Nonetheless, there still isn't a clear Supreme Court decision specifically addressing the Citizenship Clause's application to babies born of illegal immigrants.

Because of this ambiguity in Supreme Court case law, those who oppose birthright citizenship for the babies of illegal immigrants have attempted to reverse modern practice recognizing their citizenship by either proposing constitutional amendments to exclude them or passing statutes designed to trigger explicit Supreme Court resolution of the ambiguity. The former approach has been attempted several times, with no success. Constitutional amendments are difficult to enact, requiring support by two-thirds of both houses of Congress and ratification by three-quarters of the states. The latter approach is obviously easier and appears to be the focus of recent efforts by Tea Party members and others who want to exclude illegal aliens' children from birthright citizenship.

The strongest effort thus far has been undertaken in Arizona, where in January 2011, a group of Republican state legislators introduced legislation designed trigger a test case on the applicability of the Citizenship Clause to illegal immigrants' children. The proposed legislation – which was reported out of a Senate committee in late February 2011 – would, if enacted, create two different types of birth certificates in Arizona: one type for children of citizens and the other for the children of noncitizens. The expectation is that such dual birth certificates will anger immigrant groups who will challenge the law as violative of the Citizenship Clause. From a constitutional perspective, a two-tiered birth certificate approach is also likely to trigger Equal Protection Clause objections, as the Supreme Court has generally considered laws that make alienage distinctions to be presumptively unconstitutional.

Whatever the ultimate fate of Arizona's law, one thing is certain: the debate will continue to receive attention through the 2012 presidential election. The Tea Party movement appears earnest in its desire to debate immigration issues, believing that controlling illegal immigration is an important component both to improving the economy and preserving U.S. sovereignty. Even in the sensitive area of constitutional rights under the Citizenship Clause, a significant number of Americans seem to agree with this aspect of the Tea Party agenda. According to a May 2010 poll by NBC, MSNBC, and Telemundo, Americans are deeply ambivalent about citizenship for illegal immigrants' children, with a plurality of Americans (49 percent) believing their birthright citizenship should continue, but 46 percent believing it should be discontinued.

2. *The Arizona Immigration Law*

The single largest group of illegal immigrants to the United States is Mexicans, who account for 58 percent of the total. This explains why states like Arizona – a border state – have seen fit in recent months to enact tougher state laws designed to deter illegal immigration. Indeed, the Arizona law has become a lightning rod for passionate disagreements about how to reform U.S. immigration law, so it's worth examining in some detail. The Arizona law, S.B. 1070, was enacted in early 2010 and declares, "For any lawful contact made by a law enforcement official or agency ... where reasonable suspicion exists that the person is an alien who is unlawfully present in the United States, a reasonable attempt shall be made, when practicable, to determine the immigration status of the person." The Arizona law thus requires (1) "lawful contact" between an Arizona officer and individual, (2) "reasonable suspicion" that the individual is an illegal alien, and (3) a reasonable attempt to ascertain the individual's immigration status. Section 2(B) of S.B. 1070 further states that if a law enforcement officer is presented with a valid driver's license, state or tribal identification card, or other form of identification that requires proof of citizenship before issuance, the officer must presume that the person is not an illegal alien.

The Arizona law gives Arizona officers the power to inquire about immigration status whenever they have lawful contact with someone. Immigration status can be inquired into only when an individual is stopped or arrested consistent with the laws and Constitution. The net effect of the Arizona law is that if someone is lawfully stopped or arrested for something like breaking and entering or running a red light, the Arizona police can ask to see identification creating a presumption of legal status, such as a driver's license. It does not give Arizona officers power to stop or arrest someone simply because they "look" illegal or speak Spanish, contrary to media reports.

The hyperbole associated with the Arizona law has been nothing short of mind boggling. The worst sort of demagoguery has been used by the opponents of this law, who have asserted that it is racist, discriminatory, and analogous to Nazi Germany. The archbishop of the Los Angeles archdiocese, Roger Mahony, has called S.B. 1070 a "mean-spirited" reversion to "German Nazi and Russian Communist techniques." The Mexican American Legal Defense Fund called it "an open invitation to racial discrimination." Columnist Cynthia Tucker of the *Atlanta Journal-Constitution* said that S.B. 1070 "harkens back to apartheid." And a ranting *Huffington Post* op-ed by Bart Motes called it "a dumb, emotional product of cultural politics designed to appeal to the lowest common denominator of fear" that "will accomplish the goal of making the lives of select non-white Arizonans miserable."

It's not just pundits or special-interest groups using this sort of rhetoric; it includes world leaders. In his May 2010 visit to the United States, Mexican President Felipe Calderón blasted the law as "discriminatory," asserting that it required "racial profiling" and violated "any sense of human rights." Mexico subsequently issued a travel advisory, warning Mexicans not to visit Arizona. Even President Obama declared the Arizona law "troublesome" because "[i]n the United States of America, no law-abiding person, be they an American citizen, a legal immigrant or a visitor or tourist from Mexico, should ever be subject to suspicion simply because of what they look like." Notice that President Obama never even mentions "illegal" immigrants in his statement, instead referring to "law-abiding person[s]" and "legal" immigrants and "visitor[s] or tourist[s] from Mexico." All of this is typical of progressive rhetoric: a refusal to even acknowledge that individuals who cross the borders illegally are criminals. As with the war on terror – in which the *t* word is assiduously avoided, progressives prefer to refer to illegal immigrants as "undocumented" or having simply "overstayed their visas." Even Homeland Security Secretary Janet Napolitano told CNN's John King in April 2009 that "crossing the border is not a crime per se. It's civil." Yet under section 1325 of Title VIII of the U.S. Code, any alien who "enters or attempts to enter the United States at any time or place other than as designated by immigration officers" is subject to civil fine as well as imprisonment for six months to two years.

Rhetoric about racism aside, does the Arizona law serve any reasonable objective? Supporters of the law claim that its genesis lies in three words: *federal government failure* – specifically, its failure to secure the border and enforce existing federal immigration laws.

Arizona has one of the fasting-growing illegal immigrant populations in the United States. Its illegal immigrant population is currently around five hundred thousand of a total population of 6.5 million. Increasingly, those individuals crossing the Mexican border are smuggling drugs, not seeking a better life in the United States. Competition for the lucrative U.S. drug market among Mexican drug cartels has escalated sharply in recent years, increasing both traffic and violence along the U.S.-Mexican border. The murder of Arizona rancher Rob Krentz by what sheriff's authorities believed was an illegal alien involved in drug smuggling led the normally docile Arizona Cattle Growers' Association to develop the Restore Our Border Security Plan, which prefaces its suggestions for immigration reform with the following statement: "The U.S./Mexico border in southern Arizona has become a lawless region. Criminals, bandits and an international organized crime unit are operating with impunity in the region." This characterization was confirmed by a February 2011 comment by the spokesperson for U.S. Customs and Border Protection, who told the *Washington Post* that the danger faced by border patrol agents has increased "exponentially" because many of those crossing the border are involved in drug trafficking and other crimes and consequently are "much more desperate, and they have a tendency to be a lot more combative."

The federal government's inability or disinterest in stemming the flow of illegal border crossings has been noticed by Americans. A Fox News poll from July 2010 found that almost three-quarters of Americans (72 percent) believe that the federal government is not enforcing existing laws against illegal immigration. Moreover, as a February 2011 Rasmussen poll revealed, two-thirds of Americans believe that states like Arizona should have the right to enforce immigration laws if the federal government does not.

Yet clearly not all Americans think illegal immigration should be stopped. Many politically progressive cities around the country – including Los Angeles; San Francisco; New York; Washington, D.C.; Chicago; Portland; Houston; and San Diego – have enacted explicit sanctuary ordinances giving illegal immigrants safe harbor from deportation by prohibiting local law enforcement officers from inquiring about an arrestee's immigration status. In such sanctuary cities, the decision has been purposefully to look away, ignoring known illegal status, effectively transforming illegal status into legal.

Failing to check immigrant status makes zero sense from the perspective of keeping communities safe. According to Immigration and Customs Enforcement (ICE), nine hundred thousand aliens are arrested each year. If an illegal alien is arrested for a serious crime in a sanctuary city – say, assault – his or her arrest and subsequent conviction will never be reported to federal ICE officials. Once he or she serves the sentence (which may not include any jail time), the alien is free to roam the streets again, without fear of deportation. This has happened in many situations, such as the case of Rony Aguilera, a teenage illegal immigrant from Honduras. Aguilera was arrested for assault in San Francisco, a sanctuary city, in 2007 but never reported to ICE. A year after his initial arrest, Aguilera brutally murdered fourteen year-old Ivan Miranda, nearly decapitating him with a sword. If Aguilera had been reported to ICE back in 2007, Miranda might still be alive today.

The political left's support for illegal immigrant sanctuary has become so ardent that many such jurisdictions refuse to participate in ICE's Secure Communities initiative, whereby local communities submit the fingerprints of all arrestees – not just brown-skinned ones or those with accents – to be checked against a computer database containing both FBI and Homeland Security records. Secure Communities allows local law enforcement to know when an arrestee has a criminal record. Although running a fingerprint check for all arrestees makes sense generally, it makes particular sense in the context of fighting illegal immigration, as illegal immigrants tend to use numerous aliases and fake Social Security numbers. Communities that don't permit the fingerprint check – such as sanctuary cities – can often find it difficult to ascertain the true identity of someone who gives them false identification. They may not realize that the person they just arrested has been arrested twelve times before, possibly for violent crimes. But fingerprints don't lie. As Sherriff Larry Campbell of Leon County, Florida, stated, "The use of Secure Communities means criminal aliens can no longer hide behind a long list of aliases."

So what could be controversial about checking fingerprints of all arrestees to see whether they have a criminal record? A slew of communities has rejected the Secure Communities program, ostensibly because checking arrestees' backgrounds will amplify tension between police and immigrant communities and "destroy families" when arrested loved ones' criminal pasts are discovered, leading to deportation. Such thinking led Democrat Governor Pat Quinn of Illinois to halt any further expansion of Secure Communities in his state. Similarly, Washington State refused to sign a Secure Communities agreement, and cities like San Francisco; Providence, Rhode Island; and Washington, D.C., have rescinded them in the face of mounting pressure from immigrants' rights groups.

The net effect is that in much of the country, the rule of law has been eviscerated. Violations of law are being ignored – violations that are far from victimless, as they are commonly portrayed. In addition to the violence along our border and crimes committed by illegal aliens, there are subtler but real harms caused by illegal immigration that affect the lives of thousands of Americans, even those living far away from inner cities and border areas.

To get a job in the United States, potential employees must fill out an I-9 form that requires presentation of identification documents such as driver's licenses, passports, and Social Security cards. One of the dirty little secrets about illegal immigration is that it helps fuel the identity theft industry, because many illegal aliens buy forged documents, such as Social Security cards or drivers' licenses, which allow them to steal the identities of others. Not surprisingly, Federal Trade Commission data reveals that states with high rates of illegal immigration have the highest per capita rates of identity theft in the country, with Arizona ranking first, followed by Nevada, California, Texas, and Florida.

Identity theft is a major problem and getting larger every year. About 10 million Americans have their identity stolen every year. This can cause major damage to the victim's criminal record or credit rating and keep them from getting a job, student loan, mortgage, apartment, or other credit. It could even lead to a loss of life, if medical records of the illegal immigrant are mistakenly assumed to belong to the identity theft victim. Yet existing federal law deterring identity theft by illegal aliens is virtually nonexistent. For example, in 2009 the Supreme Court, in *Flores-Figueroa v. United States*, unanimously concluded that the federal identity-theft statute could not be used against an illegal immigrant who used a false Social Security number to get a job, concluding that because the prosecution couldn't prove beyond a reasonable doubt that he knew the number he bought belonged to another person, he didn't meet the law's prohibition against "knowingly" using the "identification of another person." The net result is that, in the vast majority of cases, illegal immigrants who buy false identification documents from a third party cannot be prosecuted for identity theft. The result in *Flores-Figueroa*, though unfortunate pragmatically, was indeed correct as a matter of statutory interpretation. Most illegal immigrants are assured by document brokers that the numbers are new, made up, or belonged to someone who died, so they don't "know" for sure that the numbers belong to another living person. In theory, Congress could alter the federal identity theft statute to include "reckless" use of another person's identity, but so far it hasn't done so.

Identity theft by illegal immigrants also causes havoc with victims' taxes and Social Security. When someone steals a Social Security number, those earnings are reported to the Internal Revenue Service (IRS). If the identity thief fails to pay taxes on those earnings, the IRS can demand payment from the victim, who is left scrambling to figure out what happened. Even when the identity thief does pay taxes on his or her earnings, those "excess" earnings don't necessarily get credited to the victim's Social Security account. If the identity thief uses a mismatched name and Social Security number – in other words, a Social Security number that doesn't match the correct name – the Social Security taxes withheld on his or her earnings are put into an earnings suspense file (ESF), which the government generally gets to keep. Somewhere in the neighborhood of 10 million people each year pay taxes with mismatched names and Social Security numbers, generating about $67 billion in excess revenue every year. The amount of money going to the ESF has tripled in the past ten years. Given the amount of revenue involved, it shouldn't be surprising that the government never notifies citizens whose Social Security numbers are stolen of the known mismatch.

Given all the harms associated with illegal immigration and the federal government's look-the-other-way attitude, why not let states such as Arizona do something about it? Polls have consistently shown that the majority of Americans support both the concept of the Arizona law as well as the law itself. A Pew Research poll conducted in May 2010, for example, showed that 73 percent of respondents approved of requiring people to produce documents verifying their legal status when legally arrested or detained. Sixty-seven percent approved of detaining anyone who couldn't produce such documents. When asked specifically about the Arizona law itself – the mere mention of which triggers an emotional response in many – a June 2010 ABC News and *Washington Post* poll revealed that 58 percent of Americans supported it. This result was echoed in a July 2010 poll by CBS News, which found that 57 percent of Americans thought that the Arizona law is "about right" in the way it addresses illegal immigration, and an additional 17 percent thought that the Arizona law didn't "go far enough." National popularity of the Arizona law has spawned copycat legislation that is advancing in the legislatures of many states, including Florida, Georgia, Kansas, Oklahoma, and South Carolina.

The ability of these other states to follow in Arizona's footsteps will depend on the outcome of lawsuits filed by the Obama administration against the Arizona law. In these lawsuits, the administration asserts that the S.B. 1070 is "preempted" by federal immigration law pursuant to the Supremacy Clause of Article VI of the Constitution. This means that federal immigration law is "supreme law of the land," and Arizona's law "conflicts" with federal law, requiring its invalidation. Specifically, the Obama administration contends that the Arizona law "conflicts with federal law because it necessarily imposes substantial burdens on lawful immigrants in a way that frustrates the concern of Congress for nationally-uniform rules governing the treatment of aliens throughout the country – rules designed to ensure 'our traditional policy of not treating aliens as a thing apart.'"

The first court ruling on the constitutionality of S.B. 1070 occurred in July 2010, when federal trial judge Susan Bolton issued a preliminary injunction, preventing implementation of the most contentious portions of S.B. 1070. In her opinion, Judge Bolton reasoned that the government was likely to ultimately succeed on the merits of its preemption argument, because requiring Arizona law enforcement officers to check the immigration status of arrested persons imposed burdens on their liberty that Congress would not likely have intended when enacting national immigration law. It's important to realize that Judge Bolton didn't actually rule on the merits of the Obama administration's preemption claims; she merely ruled that it was "likely to succeed on the merits" of those claims, thus warranting the issuance of a preliminary injunction until those merits could actually be addressed.

Arizona Governor Jan Brewer appealed Judge Bolton's preliminary injunction to the U.S. Court of Appeals for the Ninth Circuit – one of the most liberal circuits in the country. In April 2011, a divided three-judge panel agreed 2–1 with Judge Bolton, refusing to lift the preliminary injunction. This isn't particularly surprising, as the Court of Appeals was operating under a very deferential standard. Legally, it could reverse Judge Bolton's decision about the preliminary injunction only if it found that she "abused her discretion" in granting it. The two-judge majority of the Ninth Circuit panel agreed that the Obama administration was likely to ultimately succeed on the merits of its preemption claim, concluding,

"Congress intended for state officers to systematically aid in immigration enforcement *only* under the close supervision of the Attorney General" (emphasis added). It further concluded that, "[b]y imposing mandatory obligations on state and local officers, Arizona interferes with the federal government's authority to implement its priorities and strategies in law enforcement, turning Arizona officers into state-directed DHS [Department of Homeland Security] agents."

The Ninth Circuit majority also did something interesting that should sound familiar after reading this chapter: it invoked the views of foreign countries in bolstering its conclusion. Specifically, the court stated that S.B. 1070 "has had a deleterious effect on the United States' foreign relations," noting that the foreign leaders of Mexico, Bolivia, Brazil, Columbia, Ecuador, El Salvador, Guatemala, Honduras, and Nicaragua had "publicly criticized Arizona's law." It also referred to "six human rights experts at the United Nations; the Secretary General and many permanent representatives of the Organization of American States; the Inter-American Commission on Human Rights; and the Union of South American Nations." The court concluded, "The foreign policy of the United States preempts the field entered into by Arizona. Foreign policy is not and cannot be determined by the several states. Foreign policy is determined by the nation as the nation interacts with other nations."

The dissenting judge on the Ninth Circuit panel, Judge Bea, noted that Congress had previously indicated its desire to have state and local law enforcement officials aid enforcement of federal immigration law by declaring in section 1373(c) of Title VIII of the U.S. Code: "The Immigration and Naturalization Service shall respond to an inquiry by a Federal, State, or local government agency, seeking to verify or ascertain the citizenship or immigration status of any individual." Judge Bea concluded that this federal law, combined with others, revealed that "Congress's intent was to provide an important role for state officers in the enforcement of immigration laws, especially as to the *identification* of illegal aliens" (emphasis in original). Regarding the majority's "foreign affairs" preemption rationale, Judge Bea asserted that "any negative effect on foreign relations caused by the free flow of immigration status information between Arizona and federal officials is not due to Arizona's law, but to the laws of Congress." He also declared that "the Executive's desire to appease foreign governments' complaints cannot override Congressionally-mandated provisions.... We do not grant other nations' foreign ministries a 'heckler's veto.'"

Judge Bea's rationale didn't carry the day, and net effect of the Ninth Circuit's ruling is that implementation of the Arizona law will continue to be blocked until a trial on the merits of the preemption claims or a possible grant of review by the U.S. Supreme Court. Unless or until such Supreme Court review occurs, the Ninth Circuit's decision will send a signal to states considering copycat laws that their efforts may ultimately prove fruitless. Arizona Governor Jan Brewer has vowed to continue the legal fight until a decision on the merits has been reached, asserting that Arizona and other states "have a sovereign right and obligation to protect their citizens and enforce immigration law in accordance with the federal statute."

Brewer is right: if the Obama administration ultimately succeeds on the merits of its preemption argument, states will be rendered powerless to help enforce federal immigration law. Because the current executive branch shows little interest in enforcing existing laws, America's borders will remain porous. Although in theory Congress could enact tougher immigration laws, there's no indication such laws would be enforced any more stridently than existing laws. More pragmatically, because pro-immigrant groups keep insisting that any immigration reform include amnesty for existing illegal aliens, a political stalemate will likely prevent opening the Pandora's box of federal immigration reform until at least after the 2012 presidential election.

The Arizona law provides a good illustration of the frustrations and concerns expressed by many Americans, including the Tea Party movement. Arizona's law is popular because it exemplifies an unusually bold attempt to defend U.S. sovereignty in the simplest of ways. Open borders are tantamount to no borders at all. The unchecked onslaught of illegal immigrants for the past few decades has diminished our country's ability to protect and provide for its own citizens. Illegal immigration presents a risk to national security – terrorists can cross the border surreptitiously or with phony documents – and overwhelms our schools, health-care system, and other social services. It is the right and duty of each state and nation to defend its citizens – this is the essence of sovereignty. A country unable (or unwilling) to do so will not be a country for long.

As the issues surrounding immigration, the war on terror and the growth of international law show, there is a dangerous, politically correct attitude among progressives that sovereignty is at best a quaint, old-fashioned novelty that's no longer relevant to modern world – like chivalry or virginity. But U.S. sovereignty isn't outdated or irrelevant; it's critically important to the country's survival. The global governance crowd seduces us with rhetoric about getting along and being a global family with shared universal values. What this really means, when stripped to its core, is that we're supposed to forget about our differences, our borders, and our Constitution. We should be willing to cede them all in the name of peace unity, or not offending people.

But the truth is that differences are good. Differences may lead to conflict – sometimes even violent conflict. Although this is unfortunate, it's unavoidable on a planet filled with people of vastly different ethnicities, religions, races, languages, and cultures. We should celebrate these differences, not deny them.

It's ironic that those who understand and tout the benefits of diversity seem to forget its value when it comes to sovereignty. But the value of diversity in the realm of sovereignty is just as great as in all other contexts. Diversity provides perspective, encourages tolerance, and values the intrinsic worth of each individual. A one-size-fits-all attitude is just as sinister for global governance as it is for the boardroom, classroom, or house of worship.

It's really rather simple: When people have choice regarding the legal regimes that bind them, they have more freedom. Globalization and other progressive efforts to dilute national sovereignty undermine our own Constitution, our own uniqueness in the world, and ultimately our freedom.

As more and more of our daily actions are subject to governance by a bureaucracy in Brussels, we will lose our ability to influence not only the content of laws themselves but also their pragmatic implementation. Political accountability will evaporate, and a democratic deficit – nay, a democratic black hole – will emerge. As our own constitutional governors – Congress, courts, and our president – lose power over us, their importance will diminish. We will respect them even less as we realize that, despite all their political posturing, they're powerless to help us anymore. In the end, there's not much left of America.

For all these reasons, as the Tea Party movement understands, defending U.S. sovereignty shouldn't require an apology.

☆ 4 ☆

Constitutional Originalism

TEA PARTIERS REVERE THE CONSTITUTION AND ITS framers. They're are often spotted carting around pocket Constitutions, studying founding-era documents such as the *Federalist Papers* and *Anti-Federalist Papers*, and citing constitutional text in ways more sophisticated than many lawyers. This zeal has led several liberal-progressive pundits and reporters to analogize Tea Party constitutional reverence to Bible study. In a July 2010 essay in *Mother Jones*, for example, Stephanie Mencimer proclaimed that Tea Partiers study the Constitution "like evangelicals study the Bible."

The Bible study comparison is initially amusing – ha-ha, there go those crazy Tea Partiers again, studying the Constitution. But on closer inspection, the Bible-study analogy – and its genesis (pardon the pun) in the liberal-progressive community – is both revealing and disturbing. If studying the Constitution is like studying the Bible, what does this imply, at least in the mind of a liberal or progressive? It means that Tea Partiers are taking the Constitution too seriously, studying it with a religiosity and fervor that is, well, a bit embarrassing. Why "study" the Bible in any serious way, progressives ponder, when it's all just a giant metaphor for basic secular truths? Does anyone really believe that the universe was created in seven days? Or that the first humans lived in a Garden of Eden and were named Adam and Eve? Such a "literal" reading of the Bible is just a waste of time.

So, too, careful study of the Constitution is considered overzealous. Does anyone really believe that due process refers to process rather than substantive rights? Or that the Tenth Amendment's statement that there are "powers...reserved to the States" means that there are powers reserved to the states? Or even that the Second Amendment's declaration that "the right of the people to keep and bear arms" means that people have a right to keep and bear arms? Such a "literal reading" of the Constitution is – like the Bible – a waste of time. It may be quaint, and slightly adorable around the margins, but it's really quite ignorant.

The repeated association of Tea Partiers' constitutional reverence with Bible study is no cute and innocent analogy, but a conscious, if implicit, condemnation of their insistence that we take the Constitution seriously and literally. The Tea Party movement – as well as most conservatives – believes the best way to honor the Constitution is by interpreting it in a meaningful way, such that its words actually mean something. If the words are infinitely capacious – capable of meaning one thing today, another thing tomorrow – why have a written constitution at all?

Tea Partiers' insistence on honoring the Constitution is the latest battle in a long-running war. Throughout American history – from the very first days of the republic – there's been an ongoing and critically important debate about the best way to interpret the Constitution. This isn't a debate about the true, "right" way to interpret the Constitution, because, frankly, the Constitution itself doesn't provide any guidance and the framers – like modern Americans – held wildly different views. The debate instead is a normative one: what's the best method of interpretation, and why is it the best? Although interpretive methodology may sound arcane – of interest only to the geekiest lawyers – in reality it has tremendous implications for our everyday lives. Every American should understand what this interpretive debate is really about, and why it matters.

Tea Partiers believe the best way to ensure that the Constitution has meaning is to interpret it in an "originalist" way. When faced with constitutional language subject to varying interpretations – such as "due process" or "equal protection" – the best interpretation is that which most closely matches the meaning ascribed by those Americans who originally ratified the relevant language. This is commonly referred to as original-meaning originalism.

Contrary to common caricatures, originalism does not require judges to be psychics capable of reading the founders' minds, nor does it require polling the founding generation to figure out what a majority of them thought about an issue (if indeed they thought about it at all). Instead, originalism requires judges to interpret the Constitution with the goal of understanding the text first and foremost, parsing the words according to their common meaning at the time they were ratified. If the text's common meaning isn't clear, judges can resort to the historical context that motivated the words to be written and ratified. What problem was the constitutional text was meant to solve?

The main alternative to originalism is the living-Constitution approach. Living constitutionalism asserts that constitutional language should be viewed as living in the sense that it has no fixed meaning but is instead fluid, open to reinterpretation according to modern preferences and norms. In the words of Woodrow Wilson (an ardent living constitutionalist and progressive), the Constitution "is accountable to Darwin, not to Newton," meaning it isn't governed by fixed principles but instead should evolve and adapt to its present surroundings. In his book *Active Liberty*, Supreme Court Justice Stephen Breyer defended living constitutionalism by declaring, "Since law is connected to life, judges, in applying a text in light of its purpose, should look to consequences, including contemporary conditions, social, industrial, and political, of the community to be affected." Look closely at what Justice Breyer is saying. It's the end results – "consequences," as he puts it – that matter in interpretation. And in assessing the relative worth of various consequences, a judge should take into account "contemporary" political, social, and industrial conditions. If adhering to the original meaning of constitutional text would result in political, social, or industrial consequences that are too harsh in modern terms, a judge should be free to reinterpret the text in a way that brings about better results.

It's not hard to understand living constitutionalism's popularity. As a simple rhetorical matter, a living Constitution certainly has greater emotional appeal than a dead one. Pragmatically, living constitutionalism is also just intellectually easier than originalism. Originalism requires extensive research and familiarity with the historical context that gave rise to the relevant constitutional text. This, in turn, requires understanding the prevailing political philosophy at the time of ratification. Originalism is, in the eyes of many, just too hard, requiring judges to master a good deal of information and set aside their own personal preferences.

Substantively, living constitutionalism offers inherent flexibility, allowing judges to unmoor the Constitution from the norms and expectations of prior generations, to achieve results deemed desirable today. A living Constitution can change by simple reinterpretation of a majority of the Supreme Court, more easily progressing with society.

Yet it's a mistake to believe that originalism offers no flexibility. Some of the most important provisions of the Constitution use vague and general words. To an originalist, these amorphous phrases are an invitation not to interpret the Constitution according to personal predilections but to roll up the sleeves and study the historical context in which the words and phrases were adopted. By immersing oneself in the times in which the words were written, one can discern broader principles that are essential to guiding future interpretation. Originalism allows the broad words in the Constitution to cover new technologies and events, but only if doing so doesn't contradict the common meaning of the words at the time they were ratified.

The Fourth Amendment's prohibition of "unreasonable" searches and seizures, for example, can easily accommodate new technologies such as wiretaps, dog sniffs, and surgical procedures that were unknown at the time the Fourth Amendment was ratified in 1791. The salient question for an originalist is merely whether such activities are reasonably analogous to the kind of search or seizure that motivated the adoption of the Fourth Amendment and, if so, whether they're unreasonable in the sense contemplated by the ratifying generation. This isn't meant to suggest that there is one true answer to these Fourth Amendment questions when new technologies are used – quite the contrary. But it is meant to suggest that the questions judges should ask are fixed, from an originalist perspective. An originalist judge wouldn't feel free to go beyond the original meaning of the Fourth Amendment's text, nor the historical context that motivated its adoption.

Under originalism, therefore, the Constitution is document that works for modern times – not because its text can be ignored or reinterpreted to fit modern preferences, but because the text itself and its underlying principles are timeless and can accommodate and deal with modern situations. When this is not the case, the founders have provided an amendment process in Article V.

So admittedly, originalism isn't as infinitely flexible as living constitutionalism. But such is arguably the price of having a written constitution. Although originalism can lead to politically unpopular results or results that seem not modern or progressive enough, it isn't the end of the world when this happens. The remedy, instead, lies with the people, who are always free to change the Constitution through the amendment process.

But compared to the freewheeling, open-ended living Constitution, originalism is a conservative doctrine. It seeks to "conserve" the Constitution as written and originally understood – at least unless and until formally amended by Article V processes. As Glenn Beck put it in his keynote speech to the Conservative Political Action Committee in 2010:

> This is the disease in America. It's not just spending, it's not just taxes, it's not just corruption. It is progressivism. And it is in both parties. It is in the Republicans and the Democrats. I mean it's – it really is. I mean, I'm so sick of hearing people say, oh, well the Republicans are going to solve it all. Really? It's just progressive-lite. ... Progressivism is the cancer in America and it is

eating our Constitution. And it was designed to eat the Constitution. To progress past the Constitution.

Progressivism is all about "progression," and change is presumed to be good. Present social and political norms are, by definition, the object of criticism and legal challenge. A written Constitution whose words represent fixed principles is anathema; it's critically important to find a way to progress past the idea of a Constitution with stable meaning.

Living constitutionalism is the most powerful device ever designed to progress past the Constitution. Stripped of all the rhetoric, a living Constitution is no constitution at all. It's an interpretive tool specifically crafted to achieve desired social and political ends as quickly as possible. In the words of the decidedly left-leaning editorial board of the *New York Times* from February 2011, "Constitutional law is political." In this worldview, politics and the Constitution are one and the same; there's no room for annoying fixed principles that get in the way. Politics is about winning, not about honoring principles embodied in words written long ago. The ends are what matter.

One of the best ways to illustrate the various benefits and burdens of living constitutionalism versus originalism is to examine the 1954 companion cases of *Brown v. Board of Education* and *Bolling v. Sharpe*, in which the Supreme Court ruled that "separate but equal" public schools were unconstitutional. In so ruling, the Supreme Court overruled its decision fifty-eight years earlier, in *Plessy v. Ferguson*.

Plessy is the constitutional equivalent of original sin. The separate-but-equal doctrine upheld in *Plessy* is nowhere mentioned in the Constitution. The *Plessy* Court created it out of whole cloth, purporting to interpret the Fourteenth

Amendment's Equal Protection Clause which says that states can't deny "any person" the "equal protection of the laws."

As a textual matter – the best starting place for any constitutional analysis in the opinion of an originalist – there's no support for the concept of separate but equal. As a matter of common sense, the historical context in which the Fourteenth Amendment was adopted – it was one of three so-called Civil War amendments – makes it clear that its congressional drafters and state ratifiers meant for the Equal Protection Clause to ensure that "the laws" treated, or protected, everyone equally, regardless of their skin color. State laws were to be color blind, not color conscious. A state law that segregated by race cannot plausibly be said to provide equal protection of the laws.

Amazingly, *Plessy* turned its back on the Equal Protection Clause's original meaning, ruling that Louisiana's racial segregation law was perfectly constitutional. Listen carefully to the Court's explanation for its decision:

> So far, then, as a conflict with the fourteenth amendment is concerned, the case reduces itself to the question whether the statute of Louisiana [requiring racial segregation of railway cars] is a reasonable regulation, and with respect to this there must necessarily be a large discretion on the part of the legislature. In determining the question of reasonableness, it is at liberty to act with reference to the established usages, customs, and traditions of the people, and with a view to the promotion of their comfort, and the preservation of the public peace and good order. Gauged by this standard, we cannot say that a law which authorizes or even requires the separation of the two races in public conveyances is unreasonable, or

more obnoxious to the fourteenth amendment than the acts of congress requiring separate schools for colored children in the District of Columbia, the constitutionality of which does not seem to have been questioned, or the corresponding acts of state legislatures.

We consider the underlying fallacy of the plaintiff's argument to consist in the assumption that the enforced separation of the two races stamps the colored race with a badge of inferiority. If this be so, it is not by reason of anything found in the act, but solely because the colored race chooses to put that construction upon it. The argument necessarily assumes that if, as has been more than once the case, and is not unlikely to be so again, the colored race should become the dominant power in the state legislature, and should enact a law in precisely similar terms, it would thereby relegate the white race to an inferior position. We imagine that the white race, at least, would not acquiesce in this assumption. The argument also assumes that social prejudices may be overcome by legislation, and that equal rights cannot be secured to the negro except by an enforced commingling of the two races. We cannot accept this proposition. If the two races are to meet upon terms of social equality, it must be the result of natural affinities, a mutual appreciation of each other's merits, and a voluntary consent of individuals.... When the government, therefore, has secured to each of its citizens equal rights before the law, and equal opportunities for improvement and progress, it has accomplished the end for which it was organized, and performed all of the functions respecting social advantages with which it is endowed.... If the civil and political rights of both races be equal, one cannot be inferior to the other civilly or politically. If one race be inferior to the other socially, the constitution of the United States cannot put them upon the same plane.

It's important to dissect *Plessy*'s reasoning carefully. The *Plessy* Court concludes that Louisiana's segregation law is a reasonable means to maintain public order in the face of existing widespread racial animosity. As such, the Louisiana law was entitled to a certain degree of deference. The Court acknowledged, however, that Mr. Plessy could overcome this deference if he convinced them that the law was motivated by racial animosity. The Court rejected the animosity argument, concluding that any inferiority felt by blacks was "solely because the colored race chooses to put that construction upon it." The Court was simply unwilling to find that state-mandated segregation was either motivated by, or caused feelings of, inferiority. Without inferiority, there could be no inequality. And without inequality, there could be no violation of the Equal Protection Clause.

This is the whole of the *Plessy* analysis. Now ask yourself, Was *Plessy* an originalist or a living-Constitution interpretation of the Equal Protection Clause? The Court doesn't even mention what the clause may have meant to the members of the Thirty-Ninth Congress who proposed it or the American people who ratified it. Indeed, the only analysis *Plessy* undertakes – if one can really even call it analysis – is (1) to mention that racial segregation still existed in public schools (although the Court admits it had never been constitutionally challenged), (2) that Louisiana's law seemed geared toward preserving public order, and (3) that social relations between the races were presently strained and could be improved only with time and understanding. All three of these considerations, when parsed carefully, are living-constitutionalist justifications for upholding the separate-but-equal doctrine. They all invoke "modern norms and preferences" to justify a result that seemed morally acceptable to the *Plessy* Court at that particular moment in history. There is not one iota of evidence that the *Plessy* decision was grounded in originalism.

The only Supreme Court Justice to dissent in *Plessy* was John Marshall Harlan, a Kentucky native and former slave owner. Harlan's dissent discussed the history and meaning of all three Civil War amendments – the Thirteenth, Fourteenth, and Fifteenth Amendments. He believed the Thirteenth Amendment (outlawing slavery and involuntary servitude) and Fourteenth Amendment together, "if enforced according to their true intent and meaning, will protect all the civil rights that pertain to freedom and citizenship." Under this original meaning, Harlan asserted, "Our constitution is colorblind, and neither knows nor tolerates classes among citizens. In respect of civil rights, all citizens are equal before the law. The humblest is the peer of the most powerful. The law regards man as man, and takes no account of his surroundings or his color when his civil rights as guaranteed by the supreme law of the land are involved."

Justice Harlan wasn't trying to interpret the Constitution to make it comport with modern norms and preferences, the way the majority was. He wasn't trying to impose his own views on the country or the Constitution the way living constitutionalists do. Indeed, Harlan's own racism was clear, "The white race deems itself to be the dominant race in this country. And so it is, in prestige, in achievements, in education, in wealth, and in power. So, I doubt not, it will continue to be for all time, if it remains true to its great heritage, and holds fast to the principles of constitutional liberty." But despite Harlan's own personal views of the superiority of the white race, he wasn't willing to interpret the Constitution to reflect them. He recognized that his job as a judge was to enforce the law as written.

Harlan's dissent was an originalist dissent, and if it had been the majority opinion rather than a lone dissent, this country would have avoided many decades of shameful, state-imposed racial segregation. But the majority of the Court in *Plessy* wasn't ready or willing to go along with Harlan's originalist interpretation of the Fourteenth Amendment. Doing so would have meant that Jim Crow laws were unconstitutional, and possibly also private discrimination by owners of public accommodations such as schools, transportation, restaurants, and hotels. Perhaps the *Plessy* Court thought that enforcing the original meaning of the amendment would be too drastic. After all, as a condition to reentering the Union, Southern states were required to ratify the Fourteenth Amendment. So they ratified it, but this didn't mean they really wanted it. Declaring state-mandated segregation unconstitutional might sufficiently anger the Southern states that they'd rebel again, further imperiling an incredibly fragile, exhausted Union. It wasn't until after World War II, when the integration of the military helped change racial attitudes, that support for racial integration became widespread.

Whatever the motivation of the *Plessy* Court, its embarrassing interpretation of the Fourteenth Amendment stood for more than fifty years. *Brown v. Board of Education* finally overruled *Plessy* in 1954, holding that segregation of state public schools violated the Equal Protection Clause. The *Brown* decision was undoubtedly based on a living-constitutionalist philosophy: "In approaching this problem, we cannot turn the clock back to 1868 when the [Fourteenth] Amendment was adopted, or even to 1896 when *Plessy v. Ferguson* was written. We must consider public education in the light of its full development and its present place in American life throughout the Nation. Only in this way can it be determined if segregation in public schools deprives these plaintiffs of the equal protection of the laws." The Court then concluded that, on the basis of recent social science studies showing that black children preferred to play with white dolls, separating children "solely because of their race generates a feeling of inferiority as to their status in the community that may affect their hearts and minds in a way unlikely ever to be undone.... Whatever may have been the extent of psychological knowledge at the time of *Plessy v. Ferguson*, this finding is amply supported by modern authority. Any language in *Plessy v. Ferguson* contrary to this finding is rejected. We conclude that in the field of public education the doctrine of 'separate but equal' has no place. Separate educational facilities are inherently unequal."

The brevity of the *Brown* Court's analysis – like *Plessy* before it – is typical of living constitutionalism. After all, why bother sloshing through pages and pages of debates and discussion about what those who wrote and ratified the text thought it meant, when all that really matters is what We the Judges think the Constitution should mean today? It's much easier and faster to cite a few modern social scientists or other indicia of modern norms and be done with it.

The substantive weakness of the *Brown* analysis is apparent: if current social science studies showed that black children preferred playing with black dolls – or that post-integration, black children's feelings of inferiority increased – would the feeling-of-inferiority rationale mandate that *Brown* be overturned? What if social science studies were mixed, with some studies reaching different results? Would living-constitutionalist judges simply pick which study they thought was best, altering the Constitution accordingly?

On a broader conceptual plane, what, if anything, does a black child's preference for playing with white dolls have to do with segregation of public schools? Consider a similar hypothetical, relating to gender rather than race: What would happen if a handful of social science studies showed that boys preferred playing with Barbie over Ken? Would this suggest that boys considered themselves inferior to girls? And if this is a reasonable inference, would it also be reasonable to infer that this sense of inferiority was due to gender segregation of public bathroom facilities? If so, would this mean that gender integrated public bathrooms were required by the Equal Protection Clause? If studies showed different results ten years later, would the meaning of the Constitution then change again, allowing resegregation of public bathrooms?

It's hard to offer such criticisms of *Brown*. *Brown* isn't just iconic to the political left – it's sacrosanct. Although the left accuses Tea Partiers and conservatives of worshipping or idolatrizing the Constitution, the same can be said of progressive and liberal worship of *Brown*. It's become a symbol of the living constitutionalism movement. How could the United States ever have achieved racial integration, it's argued, unless the Supreme Court was willing to employ a living Constitution approach in *Brown* and *Bolling*? For example, during her Senate Judiciary confirmation hearings, Supreme Court Justice Elena Kagan said the outcome in *Brown* – desegregation of public schools – was "incompatible" with originalism. Similarly, former Justice David Souter proclaimed at a recent Harvard commencement speech:

For those whose exclusive norm for constitutional judging is merely fair reading of language applied to facts objectively viewed, *Brown* must either be flat-out wrong or a very mystifying decision.... [I]f *Plessy* was not wrong, how is it that *Brown* came out so differently?... Actually, the best clue to the difference between the cases is the dates they were decided, which I think lead to the explanation for their divergent results.... Did the judges of 1954 [in *Brown*] cross some limit of legitimacy into law making by stating a conclusion that you will not find written in the Constitution? Was it activism to act based on the current meaning of facts that at a purely objective level were about the same as *Plessy*'s facts 60 years before?

But living constitutionalism wasn't the only way to declare state-mandated racial segregation unconstitutional. Not only does the phrase "equal protection of the laws" suggest this is so, but so does the historical context surrounding these words' adoption.

In a 1995 article in the *Virginia Law Review*, Professor Michael McConnell demonstrated that the Thirty-Ninth Congress that proposed the Fourteenth Amendment in 1866 intended the Equal Protection Clause to outlaw racial segregation in public accommodations, including public schools. In a careful survey of congressional debates immediately following ratification of the Fourteenth Amendment, McConnell showed that majorities – and at times supermajorities – of both houses of the Thirty-Ninth Congress voted in favor of abolishing public school segregation. Such legislation was not just pie-in-the-sky attempts to do the right thing but was, in fact, a conscious effort by the Thirty-Ninth Congress to invoke its newfound authority under section 5 of the Fourteenth Amendment, which states, "The Congress shall have power to enforce, by appropriate legislation, the provisions of this article."

But because of filibusters and other procedural tactics, these anti-school-segregation proposals never became law. Yet supermajoritarian support by the Thirty-Ninth Congress – the very same Reconstruction Republicans who had proposed the Fourteenth Amendment to the states for ratification – provides strong evidence that such Republicans believed that separate but equal was inherently incompatible with the freshly ratified Fourteenth Amendment.

Unfortunately, McConnell's research came late to the intellectual party. In the intervening forty years between *Brown* and McConnell's originalist defense of the result in *Brown*, the political left insisted that living constitutionalism – and only living constitutionalism – could have been used to desegregate the public schools. It's a perception that still lingers today. Unless one has read McConnell's article, or personally conducted the same research, pouring over the debates of the Thirty-Ninth Congress that proposed the Fourteenth Amendment, one simply would not be aware of the possibility of an originalist defense of the result in *Brown*.

But of course few people will ever do either of these things. Even law students and practicing lawyers are highly unlikely to ever do these things. The progressive and liberal spin on *Brown* has become deeply entrenched, and it is virtually impossible to convince anyone on the political left to open their minds to the possibility that school desegregation could've been accomplished using an originalist interpretation of the Equal Protection Clause.

An originalist approach would not have allowed *Brown*'s companion case, *Bolling v. Sharpe*, to be decided the same way. *Bolling* was essentially the same case as *Brown* with one critical factual distinction: the law mandating public school segregation in *Bolling* was a law enacted by the District of Columbia, not a state. This seemingly small factual distinction is actually quite important. The Equal Protection Clause of the Fourteenth Amendment applies only to the states – it says "no State shall" violate equal protection. Because the District of Columbia is not, by definition, a state but a special district controlled exclusively by Congress, the public school system of the District of Columbia is not subject to the Equal Protection Clause and the Supreme Court in *Bolling* couldn't rely on it, at least not with a straight face.

As much as living constitutionalists are kosher with ignoring plain text, there are some pragmatic, political limits. For example, Article II of the Constitution says, "No person . . . shall be eligible to [the presidency] who shall not have attained the age of thirty five years, and been fourteen years a resident within the United States." Although there may be some small room for debate about whether thirty-five years old includes time in the womb or the like, it would be impossible to argue that a thirty-year-old could, consistent with the Constitution, serve as president.

A living constitutionalist could theoretically argue that the age requirement for president is anachronistic and should be completely ignored. But pragmatically, this kind of argument wouldn't pass most folks' laugh test. It doesn't take a degree in law or history to know what it means to be thirty-five years old. In the specific context of *Bolling*, there wasn't any room for legitimate debate about what the word *State* meant in the

Equal Protection Clause. No one thought or argued that it included the District of Columbia.

So if the *Bolling* Court thought it was imperative to reach the "right" result at all costs, it had to find some constitutional provision other than the Equal Protection Clause. What the *Bolling* Court chose to rely on was the Due Process Clause of the Fifth Amendment, which does textually apply to the federal government. But this is an odd use of the Due Process Clause to say the least. What is it, exactly, about public school segregation that deprives children of "life, liberty, or property, without due process of law"?

Here's the *Bolling* Court's terse explanation:

> Although the Court has not assumed to define "liberty" with any great precision, that term is not confined to mere freedom from bodily restraint. Liberty under law extends to the full range of conduct which the individual is free to pursue, and it cannot be restricted except for a proper governmental objective. Segregation in public education is not reasonably related to any proper governmental objective, and thus it imposes on Negro children of the District of Columbia a burden that constitutes an arbitrary deprivation of their liberty in violation of the Due Process Clause. In view of our decision that the Constitution prohibits the states from maintaining racially segregated public schools, it would be unthinkable that the same Constitution would impose a lesser duty on the Federal Government.

But it wasn't really "unthinkable." The Fourteenth Amendment contained an Equal Protection Clause because it was an attempt, after the Civil War, to end slaveholding states' abuses of the civil rights of slaves and abolitionists. The textual and contextual target of the Fourteenth Amendment was the states, not the District of Columbia. Maybe the framers of the Fourteenth Amendment should have mentioned the District of Columbia. But it would have been odd, considering the fact that Congress passed a law in 1862 (six years before ratification of the Fourteenth Amendment) that effectively outlawed slavery in the District.

No decision before *Bolling* had ever conceived that segregation in public schools had anything to do with the word *liberty* in the Due Process Clause or that segregation laws enacted in the normal procedural way deprived schoolchildren of liberty without due process. Indeed, such a broad, substantive conceptualization of due process – an inherently oxymoronic concept – could render virtually any ordinary law unconstitutional.

Look closely at the *Bolling* Court's rationale again: Segregation is "not reasonably related to any proper governmental objective" so it "constitutes an arbitrary deprivation of their liberty in violation of the Due Process Clause." If the Due Process Clauses – presumably of either the Fifth or Fourteenth Amendments – give the judiciary power to declare statutes unconstitutional anytime judges think the law isn't "reasonably related" to a "proper governmental objective," then virtually any law, at any moment, could be declared unconstitutional. This creates an unstable legal regime, and for that reason such an approach has been condemned. For example, a unanimous Supreme Court in *Ferguson v. Skrupa* (1963) declared: "The doctrine ... that due process authorizes courts to hold laws unconstitutional when they believe the legislature has acted unwisely – has long since been discarded. We have returned to the original constitutional proposition that courts do not substitute their social and economic beliefs for the judgment of legislative bodies, who are elected to pass laws."

Moreover, if the Due Process Clause really has such a broad substantive scope, it swallows much of the rest of the Bill of Rights as well as the rest of the Fourteenth Amendment, rendering them superfluous. A law infringing free speech, for example, could be considered by some judges to lack a "reasonable" relationship to a "proper" governmental objective. Same goes for a law restricting religious practices, regulating gun ownership, authorizing wiretaps, and so on. If the Due Process Clause provides a legitimate constitutional basis for invalidating such laws, there would be no need for the First, Second, or Fourth Amendments. Likewise, there would be no need for the Equal Protection Clause of the Fourteenth Amendment, because any law that treats people differently for no good reason would violate their liberty under the Due Process Clause.

The bottom line is that, unlike *Brown*, there's no plausible originalist interpretation that would've supported the outcome of *Bolling*. Reaching the morally right result – desegregating D.C. public schools – could have been accomplished in only one of two legitimate ways: (1) amending the Constitution to add an Equal Protection Clause that binds the federal government or (2) convincing Congress to pass an ordinary law prohibiting segregation in the D.C. public schools. The former would have required a supermajoritarian, national political consensus; the latter would have required majority support in Congress.

Both of these political means of accomplishing the morally desired result were mooted by the *Bolling* Court's living-Constitution interpretation of the Due Process Clause. That's too bad, from the standpoint of democracy. It pretermitted deliberation through the normal political process, as living constitutionalism inherently does. The second option in particular – convincing Congress to outlaw segregation in D.C. schools – would've been highly likely within a short time after *Brown*. So although an originalist interpretation would not have allowed *Bolling* to turn out the same way, the political process would have.

The big problem with *Bolling* is that even though it's morally justifiable, it's not legally justifiable. This is the problem with living constitutionalism generally. It bypasses the political process and gives judges the breathtaking power to contort the text of the Constitution to reach results they deem morally right.

Americans should pause at this realization. Assuming that desegregating D.C. public schools was the right result – an assumption I think virtually all modern Americans would agree with from a moral standpoint – does this mean that nine unelected, appointed-for-life Supreme Court Justices should have carte blanche to do whatever needed to reach "right" results? Even if you think the answer is yes, how do the Justices know what the right thing to do is? Should they just follow their own hearts? Read the latest polls? Ask God for divine guidance?

The larger point is that living constitutionalism, with its myopic fixation on results, assumes that the only people who can be relied on to "do the right thing" are the left-leaning Justices on the Supreme Court. The rest of We the People are presumably too ignorant, mean-spirited, or indifferent to moral suasion. The assumption, in other words, is that the right results can be reliably achieved only by doing an end run around the political process.

Such elitism is inherent in living constitutionalism. Our republican form of government cannot be relied on for "big," cutting-edge issues because We the People, and our elected representatives, aren't progressive enough. If ordinary people aren't ready to desegregate schools or legalize abortion, sodomy, or same-sex marriage, the progressive intelligentsia needs a mechanism to bypass our republican form of government and hand the issue off to another, more "educated" group. Living constitutionalism is the perfect solution.

There is significant force, however, to the argument that political processes rarely yield morally just results for minority groups. Any minority group – be it racial, ethnic, religious, or even political – is by definition relatively powerless in a majority-rules political system. This is why the Constitution protects various individual rights against majoritarian oppression. But the salient question, from the perspective of originalism, isn't whether, say, ending segregation in public schools was the "right" thing to do in 1954 but whether such segregation was unconstitutional. This, in turn, requires careful attention to the text of the Constitution and the historical context in which the relevant text was ratified.

Unfortunately, *Brown* and *Bolling* have become the poster children for living constitutionalism. If you dare to criticize either case, hold onto your hat. You'll be accused of secretly disagreeing with their results, harboring racist tendencies, and wanting to turn back the clock. The political left ardently believes that neither *Brown* nor *Bolling* could have come out the same way using originalism (and they're right about *Bolling*). Consequently, originalists are viewed with skepticism. Originalist judges would've never done the "right" thing in these cases – they would've let segregation go on and on and on.

Perhaps we shouldn't be surprised that the political left equates criticism of *Brown* and *Bolling* with disliking their results. After all, it's natural for living constitutionalists to think that personal beliefs and law are indistinguishable. The Supreme Court simply had to rule public school segregation unconstitutional, and it didn't much matter what logical contortions were needed to reach this result. The fact that *Brown* relied on the Equal Protection Clause while *Bolling* relied on the Due Process Clause only underscores the severity of this do-whatever-it-takes mentality.

The net result of all this nonsense is a bifurcated, us-versus-them view of the world, in which progressives insist that originalists are secret racists. And because originalists, by definition, revere the founders, the founders must be dismissed as racists, too. It's not enough to just trash originalists because originalism seems so commonsensical to most Americans. No, to really win the hearts and minds of ordinary Americans, the political left has to convince us that honoring the original meaning of the Constitution requires honoring of the flawed views of flawed men.

If We the People can be convinced the founders were racist, sexist bastards, we won't want to revere either them or their pesky Constitution. Why should we give a hoot about what a bunch of backward founders thought about things? Modern, enlightened Americans shouldn't feel constrained, the argument goes, by the political philosophy of a bunch of dead, racist, sexist white guys.

We have all heard this refrain in the mainstream media, and probably also from the mouths of our left-leaning teachers and professors. Popular denigration of the founders has become commonplace, feeding a mind-set that is critical to shaping the debate about constitutional law. In 1987, at a bicentennial celebration of the Constitution, the first African American Supreme Court Justice, Thurgood Marshall, had this to say about the founders:

> I do not believe that the meaning of the Constitution was forever "fixed" at the Philadelphia Convention. Nor do I find the wisdom, foresight, and sense of justice exhibited by the Framers particularly profound. To the contrary, the government they devised was defective from the start, requiring several amendments, a civil war, and momentous social transformation to attain the system of constitutional government, and its respect for the individual freedoms and human rights, we hold as fundamental today.

Marshall's argument is that the original Constitution – which lacked a Bill of Rights, freedom for blacks and other important things – was fundamentally "defective," explaining why a living Constitution is preferable to an originalist one.

Columbia law professor Michael Dorf described living constitutionalism this way: "For living Constitutionalists, the act of ratification by people who are long dead, and whose numbers did not include any women or enslaved African-Americans, does not suffice to make the Constitution effective today." Harvard law professor Michael Klarman similarly told students gathered at a recent Constitution Day event at Johns Hopkins University, "The Framers' constitution, to a large degree, represented values we should abhor or at least reject today.... [I]t's hard to celebrate a Constitution that explicitly guaranteed the return of fugitive slaves to their masters, protected the international slave trade for 20 years, and enhanced the South's national political representation to reflect slaveholding."

It's not just liberal legal intellectuals who denigrate the founders and the Constitution they created. Listen to how Conor Cruise O'Brien, a contributing editor of the *Atlantic*, spoke of Thomas Jefferson, the author of the Declaration of Independence, and what he called the "cult of the founding fathers":

> Thomas Jefferson was demonstrably a racist, and a particularly aggressive and vindictive one at that.... I believe that in the next century, as blacks and Hispanics and Asians acquire increasing influence in American society, the Jeffersonian liberal tradition, which is already intellectually untenable, will become socially and politically untenable.... I believe that Jefferson will nonetheless continue to be a power in America in the area where the mystical side of Jefferson really belongs: among the radical, violent, anti- federal libertarian fanatics.... Doctrinally, Jefferson is a patron saint far more suitable to white supremacists than to modern American liberals.

Notice how O'Brien sets up a bifurcated worldview: (1) progressive nonracists who understand Jefferson for the scoundrel he was and (2) violent, libertarian, white supremacists who worship Jefferson as a patron saint. Now take the typical readership of a well-respected literary magazine like the *Atlantic* and ask yourself whether those readers would want to align themselves with the second camp? Of course not, nor would anyone who doesn't typically read the *Atlantic*.

Along the same lines, MSNBC's Keith Olbermann issued a Founders' Day rant in February 2010, accusing Tea Partiers of being racist, a trait he believed they shared with the

founders: "The whole of the 'anger at government' movement is predicated on this. Times are tough, the future is
confusing, the threat from those who would dismantle our
way of life is real. . . . And the president is black. But you can't
come out and say that's why you're scared. . . . And I know
phrases like 'Tea Klux Klan' are incendiary and I know I use
them in part because I'm angry that at so late a date we still
have to bat back that racial uneasiness which envelops us all."

And as for the Tea Party's reverence of the founders,
Olbermann had this to say: "Not all of our heritage is honor-
able. Not all the decisions of the founding fathers were noble.
Not very many of the founding fathers were evolved enough
to believe that black people were actually people. The Founding Fathers thought they were and fought hard to make sure
they would always remain slaves."

Olbermann's characterization of the founders as unsavory,
backward characters with evil hearts is all too common these
days among those who self-identify as liberal or progressive.
The general thrust of modern liberal thought on the founders
is summed up in Joe Feagin's book, *Racist America: Roots,
Current Realities and Future Reparations*, in which he proclaims:

> For the founders, freedom meant protection for the
> unequal accumulation of property, particularly property
> that could produce a profit in the emerging capitalist
> system. Certain political, economic, and racial interests
> were conjoined. This [the constitutional convention of
> 1787] was not just a political gathering with the purpose
> of creating a major new bourgeois-democratic govern-
> ment; it was also a meeting to protect the racial and
> economic interests of men with substantial property
> and wealth in the colonies. As Herbert Aptheker has

put it, the Constitution was a "bourgeois-democratic government for the governing of a slaveholder-capitalist republic. . . . The new nation formed by European Americans in the late eighteenth century was openly and officially viewed as a *white* republic.

The disturbing, common theme running between all these liberal-progressive statements, from Justice Marshall to Michael Dorf, Michael Klarman, Conor O'Brien, Keith Olbermann, and Joe Feagin: reverence for the founders, and hence their flawed Constitution, is an indicia of racism. These constant assertions have serious spillover effects, even at a local level. Consider what erupted in 1997 in New Orleans, when a predominantly African American public elementary school was stripped of its controversial name – George Washington Elementary – because, in the words of one supporter of the name change, "to African-Americans, George Washington has about as much meaning as [white supremacist] David Duke."

The net result is that many ordinary Americans who self-identify as liberal or progressive sincerely, albeit ignorantly, believe that those who hold the founders or the Constitution in high esteem must secretly harbor a desire to turn back the clock to a time when slavery existed and women couldn't vote. The debate between living constitutionalism and originalism is laden with racial overtones and innuendo. It's little wonder, then, that the Tea Party's embrace of originalism and reverence for the founders invites – indeed begs for – accusation of racism by the political left.

With so much antifounder rhetoric and race baiting out there, television and radio host Glenn Beck recently felt the need to have Founders' Fridays, dedicated to educating his audience about the founders and the positive principles for which they stood. Sadly, it may be the first time many Americans have had the chance to learn anything other than cursory or negative information about the founders. From my own experience teaching law for more than fifteen years, I can attest that my own students – by definition very intelligent, successful college graduates – have little knowledge of the founders, other than vague and often inaccurate general impressions, one of which is that they were all a bunch of racist, sexist, hypocritical bastards. If Beck's high ratings for Founders' Fridays are any indication, millions of Americans hunger for a little positive reinforcement about the founders and the Constitution they gave us.

Those who embrace originalism should be able and willing to articulate two glaring flaws with the political left's automatic association of originalism with racism, sexism, and other nefarious isms. First, there is a huge difference between revering the founders versus revering the Constitution they wrote and the founding generation ultimately ratified. The Tea Party's reverence is for the Constitution and its principles, not the human beings who wrote it. Although the founders are held in high esteem, it's their vision and successful implementation of a unique governmental architecture that is admired, not their personal lives. The fact that some founders owned slaves, committed adultery, or drank too much isn't relevant to constitutional interpretation, despite the constant refrain of progressives who often suggest that such matters overshadow the Constitution itself. For originalists, it's the governmental blueprint the founders drew that matters – a blueprint made all the more impressive because, despite incessant assaults from the left, it has stood the test of time.

Second, the fact that the original, unamended Constitution ratified in 1789 acknowledged the continuation of slavery

in some states doesn't undermine the moral force of originalism at all – in fact, quite the contrary. Subsequent amendments have superseded these original provisions and are fully
entitled to interpretive respect by an originalist.

The original Constitution's provisions addressing slavery
represented gut-wrenching political compromises. It didn't
resolve the slavery question one way or another. But this
doesn't mean the Constitution was pro-slavery. At most it was
neutral and arguably, in some places, actually hostile toward
slavery. The so-called "Three-Fifths Clause of Article I, section 2, for example, apportions the House of Representatives
"by adding to the whole Number of free Persons, including those bound to Service for a Term of Years, and excluding
Indians not taxed, three fifths of all other Persons." The "other
persons" is an implicit reference to slaves. But by counting
slaves as only three-fifths of a person for apportionment purposes, the founders weren't sending a moral message that
slaves were "worth" only three-fifths of nonslaves. Instead,
three-fifths was a raw compromise between one and zero:
slaveholding states wanted slaves to count the same as nonslaves; free states didn't want to count slaves at all. In the
absence of the three-fifths compromise, slave states would
have been entitled to an even greater number of representatives in Congress.

Similarly, the 1808 Clause of Article I, section 9 declared,
"The Migration or Importation of such Persons as any of the
States now existing shall think proper to admit, shall not be
prohibited by the Congress prior to the Year one thousand
eight hundred and eight, but a tax or duty may be imposed
on such Importation, not exceeding ten dollars for each Person." Again, the reference to "such Persons" is implicitly to
slaves, and the 1808 Clause, though recognizing the existence

of slavery, is decidedly antislavery, giving Congress the power to prohibit further slave importation after 1808 – twenty years after the original Constitution's proposal. Moreover, the 1808 Clause allowed Congress to tax slave importation at a then-hefty rate of up to ten dollars per slave. The belief was that through heavy taxation and halting further importation, the institution of slavery would die a slow but steady death. Congress in fact exercised its 1808 Clause authority promptly, banning further slave importation effective January 1, 1808, the earliest possible opportunity. Under this law, the importation of slaves became an act of piracy, punishable by death.

The one provision of the original Constitution that might be characterized as pro-slavery was the Fugitive Slave Clause of Article IV, section 2. It declared, "No person held to service or labour in one state, under the laws thereof, escaping into another, shall, in consequence of any law or regulation thereof, be discharged from such service or labour, but shall be delivered up on a claim of the party to whom such service or labour may be due." The purpose of the Fugitive Slave Clause was to recognize that, although slavery had been prohibited in some states, it still existed in others. Under the new union, the Constitution also declared – just before the Fugitive Slave Clause, in Article IV, section 1 – that "Full faith and credit shall be given in each State to the public acts, records, and judicial proceedings of every other State." The Full Faith and Credit Clause formalized recognition of the validity of other states' laws. It effectively said, "We may do things differently here in New York, but we recognize the validity of Georgia's laws and court judgments."

Arguably, the Full Faith and Credit Clause alone would have required the return of escaped slaves. But there was some doubt on this score, because courts had recognized a broad exception to the clause, allowing State A to ignore State B's laws when State B's laws violated the "public policy" of State A. Inserting a special full-faith-and-credit clause for escaped slaves assuaged slaveholding states' concern that free states would undermine slavery by refusing to return escaped slaves.

The slaveholding states' concerns about free states trying to undermine slavery were well founded. Free states enacted various laws that attempted to get around the Fugitive Slave Clause, including, for example, a "personal liberty law" enacted by Pennsylvania. This law prohibited a Pennsylvania judge from issuing a certificate to return escaped slaves. In 1842, in *Prigg v. Pennsylvania*, the Supreme Court ruled 8–1 that Pennsylvania's law conflicted with the Fugitive Slave Clause and was accordingly unconstitutional. In reaching this conclusion, Justice Story's opinion declared that the Fugitive Slave Clause was a "fundamental article, without the adoption of which the Union could not have been formed." So although the Court may not have liked slavery or thought it was morally just to return an escaped slave, the plain language of the Constitution – for better or worse – allowed it to reach no other result. A living-constitutionalist Court, by contrast, would have most certainly ignored the text and historical context of the Fugitive Slave Clause and found some creative way to reach the "right" result.

All of these provisions in the original Constitution did recognize – albeit reluctantly – that slavery still existed in some states. But far from being "a covenant with death, and an agreement with hell," as abolitionist William Lloyd Garrison proclaimed, the original Constitution represented, at most, an uneasy compromise that was the pragmatic price of forming a union. The Constitution didn't solve the most troubling human rights issue of its day, but it would be a mistake to say it endorsed slavery's indefinite continuation. The standard liberal claim that the Constitution "condoned" slavery and is consequently unworthy of reverence is either an intentional lie or an ignorant falsehood.

More important, the amendments ratified immediately after the Civil War are a strong reminder that originalism has nothing whatsoever to do with reverence of the "original" Constitution. What originalists care about is the current Constitution in all its glory, not the "original" Constitution as it existed in 1789. Amendments are as much a part of Constitution as the Constitution itself – in fact, they are more important to an originalist because they were written later in time and thus can either repeal or clarify earlier constitutional language. Because the original Constitution's provisions relating to slavery were repealed or rendered moot by the Civil War amendments, they are simply no longer of any interpretive value to an originalist.

The continuing charge by the political left that originalism is secret code for racism undoubtedly scares many good meaning Americans away from originalism. But the political left's proffered alternative – living constitutionalism – is downright dangerous to the long-term health of the republic. Stripped of the rhetorical flourish about dead white hands controlling the destiny of modern Americans, living constitutionalism is subjectivism run amok. It's politics in its rawest, ugliest form, requiring only five of nine Supreme Court Justices to remake the Constitution according to their own views and life experiences. As Justice Sonia Sotomayor (then a judge on the U.S. Court of Appeals) revealed in a 2002 law journal article, "I would hope that a wise Latina woman with the richness of her experiences would more often than not reach a better conclusion than a white male who hasn't lived that life."

Sotomayor's statement is unsurprising coming from a living constitutionalist. She unapologetically accepts that her gender and ethnicity will – and should – lead her to a different conclusion from that of a white male. It's the antithesis of the idea that we are a nation of laws, and not men (or women). This foundational and stabilizing idea – that law is law, fixed and unvarying from person to person, judge to judge – simply isn't compatible with the living constitutionalist's perspective. The judge's race, gender, or ethnicity not only could influence their decisions but in fact should influence them, because the judge's job is to do the "right" thing, a determination that will naturally vary according to his or her own unique life experiences. Although variation in perspective from person to person is undeniable and inevitable, is it appropriate to consciously and proudly declare it the central consideration in constitutional interpretation? Equally important, is it appropriate to lump individuals together by broad categories such as gender, race, religion, or ethnicity and assume that membership in these categories does and should lead to the "right" constitutional results?

Although the flexibility of living constitutionalism has some appeal, the harms created far outweigh this benefit. More specifically, apart from balkanizing society by assuming individuals can be stereotyped according to the categories to which they belong, living constitutionalism creates three distinct social harms. First, it allows the judiciary to discard fundamental, structural features of Constitution – such as federalism and limited government – that were designed to protect citizens from tyrannical government. Second, it encourages political lethargy by creating an expectation that the judiciary will fix intractable political problems by doing an interpretive about-face. If the Constitution is malleable enough to change with the times (without a formal constitutional amendment), there is no need for We the People to get involved. The Court will fix the problem and we can all get on with our busy lives – taking our kids to soccer, eating our chicken nuggets, and paying our bills. And third, living constitutionalism undermines respect for the government and the rule of law by encouraging the idea that the Constitution is just another political football, a plaything of the ruling intelligentsia.

Consider the first point about discarding liberty-protecting features of the constitutional architecture. Most Americans don't know enough about the Constitution and its history to realize that concepts like federalism – so-called states' rights – and limited government were actually designed to protect individual liberty. They think the phrase "states' rights" – a phrase that embodies the Tenth Amendment's declaration that there are "powers" not given to the federal government that are "reserved to the States" – has some permanent, nefarious link to the Confederacy and slavery. Consider the February 2011 rant on a blog called *Norwegianity* that characterized states' rights as "Klassic Konservative speak for hell no we're not letting niggers vote."

The South's invocation of states' rights in its succession from the Union is far from a legitimate basis for defining the meaning of the Tenth Amendment. The South's interpretation was just that – the South's interpretation. The country fought a Civil War over this interpretation and the South lost. As a result of the Civil War, the Constitution was amended to include the Thirteenth, Fourteenth, and Fifteenth Amendments, all of which took away specific and important slices of state sovereignty. What "states' rights" meant before the Civil War amendments was therefore a very different from what it meant afterward.

The continuing association of states' rights with slavery or racism is either intentionally deceptive or simply ignorant of this constitutional history. And the Tenth Amendment itself speaks not merely in terms of powers reserved to the states but in fact says such powers are "reserved to the States respectively, *or to the people.*" This last phrase is generally forgotten, but it represents an important concept – namely that after giving certain limited powers to the federal government, and reserving other powers to the states, there were still some powers that ultimately belonged to neither government but were instead retained by the people. This reservation of "power" in the name of the people is perfectly symbiotic with the language of the preceding Ninth Amendment, which states that the "enumeration in the Constitution, of certain rights, shall not be construed to deny or disparage others retained by the people."

The unmistakable message of the Ninth and Tenth Amendments is that the people retained significant portions of available sovereignty. Unlike the British governmental structure so eloquently defended by Thomas Hobbes's *Leviathan,* the newly formed government in the United States did not lodge all sovereignty within government (whether federal or state), but instead reserved significant rights and powers to the people. And in an attempt to limit expansion of the power that was given to government, the Constitution not only enumerated the limited powers of the federal government but also made it clear, in the Tenth Amendment, that any other powers not enumerated were reserved to the states or their people.

One of the most unique and important architectural features of our Constitution was that, by dividing government power both vertically (between the federal and state governments) and horizontally (among the three branches), the resulting inter- and intragovernmental rivalries would help dampen the inherent tendency toward expansion of governmental power and tyranny over We the People. By carefully defining and dispersing governmental power, the Constitution created checks and balances to minimize the potential for our governors to abuse their power over us.

In a living-Constitution world, however, these architectural limits on governmental power can be brushed aside as anachronistic annoyances, flies buzzing around the heads of progressive, all-knowing judges. Once judges are unmoored from the constitutional text and historical context in which it was adopted, they're free to remake the nation according to their own desires, disregarding critically important concepts like limited government or federalism.

Two examples illustrate this point – one recent, the other from the New Deal era. The first example came to light in late 2010, after the Senate passed a food-safety bill that enjoyed broad bipartisan support, passing with a 73–25 vote. When the bill was forwarded to the House for consideration, the House parliamentarian – the person responsible for checking and enforcing various rules of the House – identified what's called a blue-slip problem with the bill. Blue slips effectively notify the Senate that it has violated Article I, section 7, of the Constitution, which declares, "All Bills for raising Revenue shall originate in the House of Representatives." Because a portion of the food-safety bill included fees that were considered revenue raisers, it violated the plain language the Constitution.

In the face of such a problem, the constitutionally correct response would be to start all over again, allowing the House to pass the food-safety bill first, then sending it to the Senate for passage once more. In the waning days of the 111th Congress, there simply wasn't enough time to start from scratch. Moreover, the turnover of the House of Representatives to Republican control, beginning with the new 112th Congress in January 2011, made it likely that there wouldn't be enough votes for House passage. So the Democrats, who were the chief proponents of the food-safety bill, became annoyed at the prospect of having to employ the time consuming, required constitutional process. They struggled to understand how such a technicality could stand in the way of what they believed to be the obvious "right" result – immediate passage of the law.

The political left responded to this constitutional quandary by accusing the Republicans of being obstructionist. The *Washington Monthly*, for example, articulated the situation as follows: "a Democratic procedural slip-up + Republican dickishness = more salmonella poisoning." The *New York Times* characterized the problem as an "arcane parliamentary mistake," concluding that it was part of a vast right-wing conspiracy to "block the bill along with everything else Mr. Reid is hoping to accomplish." It lamented the fact that, to pass the bill, Reid and company were being "forced to burn time jumping through all of the procedural hoops," thus "sacrific[ing] other legislative priorities." Nowhere in these statements is there recognition that the holdup was constitutional rather than political. But then again, from the perspective of the political left, constitutional law and politics are one and the same.

The brouhaha over the food-safety bill illustrates well the political left's view of the Constitution as an annoying technicality that stands in the way of progress. The portion of the Constitution that impeded passage of the food-safety bill – the

Origination Clause of Article I, section 7 – isn't a technicality any more than the Tenth Amendment or any other portion of the Constitution. The founders included the Origination Clause for a reason. Revenue raising – in other words, tax – bills must originate in the House of Representatives because the founders believed that the House would be more accountable to the people than the Senate. House members are elected every two years instead of every six, and there are a lot more Representatives than there are Senators. The basic idea was that, before raising taxes on the people, the "people's branch" – the House – should first agree. Allowing the Senate to go first, by contrast, would have created significant political pressure on the House to just go along with something desired by the Senate – as indeed was the case with the food-safety bill.

The Origination Clause was also designed to give populous states more influence over taxation, tempering the smaller states' greater influence in the Senate and ensuring again that tax measures enjoyed broad popular support. As James Madison explained in *Federalist No. 58*, "This power over the purse may, in fact, be regarded as the most complete and effectual weapon with which any constitution can arm the immediate representatives of the people, for obtaining a redress of every grievance, and for carrying into effect, every just and salutary measure."

Madison's words were prescient. The House's power over the purse, granted by the Origination Clause, can help the people "obtain redress of every grievance." To understand this in modern terms, consider the clause's potential impact on Obamacare, which continues to be unpopular. Now that the House of Representatives is dominated by Republicans – a significant number of whom self-identify as

Tea Partiers – funding for Obamacare must originate in the Republican controlled Ways and Means Committee and ultimately pass a Republican-controlled House before any further action can be taken by the Senate. Whether the House Republicans use this power to defund Obamacare remains to be seen, but it illustrates the potential power of the Origination Clause as a device to obtain redress for grievances from the people's House. Like all constitutional provisions, the Origination Clause has continuing relevancy in modern times.

The second illustration of living constitutionalism's disdain for constitutional limits on governmental power involves the famous switch in time that saved nine. That phrase refers to the Supreme Court's "reinterpretation" of the Commerce Clause during the New Deal era, a switch that saved nine, meaning the Supreme Court as a body of nine Justices. Back in the 1930s, President Roosevelt, together with a Democrat-controlled Congress, enacted a series of laws that gave the federal government unprecedented power. This legislation – collectively referred to as the New Deal – was designed to pull the United States out of the Great Depression.

In a series of early cases, the Supreme Court, employing originalist reasoning, struck down much of the New Deal, including federal minimum-wage and other labor laws, concluding that the power to regulate interstate commerce was not understood by the ratifying public to include the power to regulate the intrastate employer-employee relationship. But there was tremendous political pressure to uphold New Deal legislation – including pressure by President Roosevelt, who announced an aggressive court-packing plan that, if enacted by Congress, would have given the president significant new power to increase the size of the Supreme Court.

In the end, Justice Owen Roberts succumbed to the pressure, doing a 180-degree turnabout in his interpretation of liberty of contact. The switch occurred in 1937, in *West Coast Hotel v. Parrish*, a decision upholding the federal minimum-wage law and overruling the Court's contrary result reached just fourteen years earlier in *Adkins v. Children's Hospital*. The *West Coast Hotel* majority explained its about-face on this aspect of liberty:

> There is an additional and compelling consideration which recent economic experience has brought into a strong light. The exploitation of a class of workers who are in an unequal position with respect to bargaining power and are thus relatively defenseless against the denial of a living wage is not only detrimental to their health and well being, but casts a direct burden for their support upon the community. What these workers lose in wages the taxpayers are called upon to pay. The bare cost of living must be met. We may take judicial notice of the unparalleled demands for relief which arose during the recent period of depression and still continue to an alarming extent despite the degree of economic recovery which has been achieved. It is unnecessary to cite official statistics to establish what is of common knowledge through the length and breadth of the land. While in the instant case no factual brief has been presented, there is no reason to doubt that the state of Washington has encountered the same social problem that is present elsewhere. The community is not bound to provide what is in effect a subsidy for unconscionable employers.

The five-justice majority in *West Coast Hotel* used a living-Constitution approach to reach the desired result of upholding the minimum wage. They simply decided to reinterpret liberty because the times had changed. The "old" Constitution no longer met modern needs, so it needed to be discarded. Rather than enforcing the Commerce Clause as understood by the American public that ratified it, five Justices took it upon themselves to transform it through reinterpretation.

As *West Coast Hotel* shows, one of the worst things about living constitutionalism is that it renders ordinary Americans missing in action, cut out of the dialogue that precedes constitutional change. All we need to do, in the living-Constitution world, is convince the Supreme Court to change its mind, allowing five unelected Justices to rewrite it using modern understandings. This may be quick and convenient, but it bypasses the prolonged and widespread political engagement required for constitutional amendments under Article V. It encourages popular political lethargy, a condition undeniably dangerous to the proper functioning of our republican form of government.

It's more than a little ironic, therefore, that the political left criticizes the Tea Party for proposing various constitutional amendments and even calling for a state-initiated constitutional convention as allowed by Article V. Tea Partiers' opposition to bailouts, stimulus packages, and healthcare reform has generated substantial interest in proposing amendments to do such things as requiring a balanced budget, repealing the Sixteenth (federal income tax) and Seventeenth (direct election of Senators) Amendments, rebalancing power between the federal and state governments (the so-called Federalism Amendment), and giving states a veto power over federal laws (the so-called Repeal Amendment).

Critics of the Tea Party don't understand how Tea Partiers can simultaneously pledge fealty to the Constitution while seeking to change it. In the words of Ian Millhiser on the progressive blog *Think Progress*, such amendment proposals are akin to Tea Partiers "wrapping themselves in the rhetoric of the Constitution while simultaneously trying to remake [the] document into something completely unrecognizable." Similarly, Garrett Epps declared in an *Atlantic* essay that such proposed amendments are "dishonest madness" because they reveal that supporters of the measures, including the Tea Party, are "[b]raggarts who bray about their devotion to the Constitution [yet] want to tear it up."

These criticisms ultimately prove intellectually empty. Imagine that I have a bicycle that I love. You borrow it one day, and not revering it as much as I do, you damage its seat, handlebars, and spokes. When I look at my beloved bicycle, I am deeply saddened by these alterations. What should I do: lament the harm done, or restore the bicycle to its original glory? Of course I should restore it. This is precisely what the amendments supported by the Tea Party seek to do – restore the Constitution, not remake it.

But let's assume, for the sake of argument, that some of the Tea Partiers' proposals would change the Constitution rather than restore its original meaning. Even then, such proposals wouldn't be hypocritical or dishonest but perfectly consistent with originalism. Remember that originalism has nothing to do with revering the original, unamended Constitution. It reveres the Constitution as a whole, in its current, amended form. And because the Constitution itself, in Article V, provides for a legitimate mode of change, amendments ratified via Article V processes are not only legitimate but also entitled to equal reverence. There is, in other words, no intellectual tension between originalism and constitutional change, so long as the change occurs in the manner specified by the Constitution itself.

Any attempt to amend the Constitution through processes other than those provided in Article V – such as reinterpretation through living constitutionalism – subverts our republican form of government, signaling that We the People aren't really necessary or in control after all. And the more common amendment through reinterpretation becomes, the less respect Americans will likely have for their government.

Such declining respect is revealed by long-term polling data conducted by the Pew Research Center. In 1958, when Pew began surveying Americans about their attitudes toward the federal government, 73 percent of respondents trusted the federal government to do what is right "just about always" or "most of the time." By 2010, this percentage had declined to an abysmal 22 percent. Among Tea Partiers, the trust level is even lower, with only 7 percent always or mostly trusting the federal government to do the right thing.

Among the chief complaints of the Pew respondents, a majority (52 percent) thought the federal government is "too big and powerful." Similarly, a December 2010 Rasmussen poll revealed that only 39 percent of Americans think that the federal government currently operates within the limits established by the Constitution. So Americans clearly don't approve of the federal government's virtually unfettered growth since the New Deal. They – particularly the Tea Partiers – want their government to stay within constitutionally defined limits. In a September 2009 poll conducted by the National Constitution Center and Associated Press, three-quarters of Americans agreed with the statement,

"The United States Constitution is an enduring document that remains relevant today."

Despite such widespread reverence by ordinary Americans, living constitutionalism continues to demean and disparage the Constitution's original meaning, insisting that it's flawed and in need of amendment by judicial reinterpretation. The simultaneous rise of living constitutionalism and distrust of the federal government is not coincidental. If Americans think their input doesn't really matter, that the powers that be – intelligentsia, political class, or whatever you want to call it – will find a way to do what it wants regardless of the Constitution, it's reasonable to conclude that this would negatively affect their trust of government.

Living constitutionalism inherently implies that the American people can't be trusted to amend the Constitution via Article V or enact needed ordinary laws. This is ironic, as one of living constitutionalism's chief complaints about originalism is that it allows the dead hand of prior generations to trump the modern Americans' preferences. As it turns out, living constitutionalism does exactly this, wresting important legal questions out of modern Americans' hands (via the democratic process) and placing them in those of politically unaccountable judges.

The transfer of authority from We the People to We the Judges emits an elitist tone that has not gone unnoticed by the Tea Partiers, amplifying their distrust of the federal government. Originalism is thus viewed as a critically important way to take back control from elites and return it to the people.

Yet what makes Tea Partiers think originalism would result in better outcomes for America? As an initial matter, there appears to be something comforting in the notion of a written Constitution with a fixed meaning. If a written constitution doesn't have a fixed meaning, what would be the purpose of having a written Constitution in the first place? Thomas Jefferson presciently made this point many years ago, declaring, "Our peculiar security is in the possession of a written Constitution. Let us not make it a blank paper by construction."

Indeed, the existence of an amendment process in Article V suggests that the founders assumed the original meaning would control the judiciary's constitutional interpretation. After all, a Constitution without fixed meaning would never need to be amended; it could just be reinterpreted. Article V is thus the founders' way of telling us that the Constitution they wrote was to be honored, in good times and bad, unless and until amended. The fact that they provided a mechanism for amendment recognizes that they weren't egoists hell bent on entrenching their way of doing things. Article V allows succeeding generations of Americans to put their own unique fingerprints on our most important legal document.

If we want to change, we can – our Constitution is far from dead in the eyes of originalists. But legitimate constitutional change must come through the means explicitly outlined in Article V. This means change won't come easy – requiring supermajorities, not mere majorities, to agree. But this has happened many times. The Constitution has come a long way since it was originally ratified in 1789. The American people ratified an entire Bill of Rights – the first ten amendments – in 1791, only two short years after the original Constitution was ratified. We then ratified three critical constitutional amendments after the Civil War, accomplishing remarkable changes such as abolishing slavery, granting blacks the right to vote, and ensuring equal protection of the laws for all. We granted women (Nineteenth Amendment) and eighteen-year-olds (Twenty-Sixth Amendment) the right to vote. We instituted Prohibition (Eighteenth Amendment) in 1919, then promptly changed our minds and repealed it (Twenty-First Amendment) in 1933. In all, our Constitution has been amended twenty-seven times.

Despite the political left's claim to the contrary, the American people have shown both a willingness and ability to amend the Constitution when so desired. Although constitutional amendments are difficult, whoever said constitutional change was supposed to be easy? If it were, there wouldn't be much long-term stability in our government. Amendments require supermajorities for the simple reason that constitutionalizing things entrenches them, making them equally difficult to undo later. Once something becomes a matter of constitutional law, it's the supreme law of the land, and no further debate or experimentation is possible. Constitutional law establishes a one-size-fits-all rule that cannot be contradicted, which suggests rather strongly that Americans had better agree on the constitutional rule before it becomes fixed.

In short, constitutionalizing something takes the matter in question out of the ordinary political process, placing it beyond the control of politically accountable majorities and in the control of a politically unaccountable federal judiciary. Such foundational legal changes shouldn't be lightly undertaken, and Article V's supermajoritarian amendment process recognizes this basic reality. Living constitutionalism turns this concept on its head, allowing the Constitution to be changed through mere reinterpretation of a majority of the Supreme Court.

Originalism isn't easy. In fact, it's hard. It requires that each new generation of Americans be educated in the founding generations' political philosophy – something that simply does not happen today, even in law schools. Tea Partiers believe that it's time Americans reacquaint themselves with the constitutional text and its historical context. Without this basic education, even the most highly educated among us will be poor citizens.

Reflecting this attitude, the Tea Party–led return of Republican control of the House of Representatives in November 2010 led to swift implementation of three pro-originalism reforms. First, the newly formed Tea Party Caucus, organized by Tea Party favorite Representative Michele Bachmann of Minnesota, began sponsoring bimonthly lectures about the Constitution, open to any member. The first lecture, in late January 2011, was delivered by Justice Antonin Scalia, who advised members to get a copy of the *Federalist Papers* and keep them on their desks.

The second reform was to read the Constitution aloud from the floor of the House, something that remarkably had never been done before. In classic originalist fashion, the Republican leadership decided to read only those portions of the Constitution that hadn't been repealed by subsequent amendments. Provisions such as the Three-Fifths Clause and the prohibition amendment were not read. Democrats accused the Republican leadership of "whitewashing" and "Huck Finning" the Constitution by failing to read text that no longer has any legal force, exhibiting once again their knee-jerk association of the Constitution, and originalism, with racism.

The third and most significant pro-originalism reform implemented by the House was to implement the Enumerated Powers Act, requiring that every bill identify the specific constitutional authority relied on for the assertion of power proposed by the bill. This reform was the number-one priority of the Contract from America articulated by the Tea Party. It reflects deep frustration with Congress's previous indifference about constitutional limitations on its power. Tea Partiers' opposition to health-care reform, for example, has been motivated principally by a belief that Congress doesn't have constitutional authority to force individuals to buy a private product like health insurance.

Under the new rule, some lawmakers can be expected to cite constitutional power sources without much reflection. Others may take it more seriously. Indeed, the symbolic value could be significant, reminding members of Congress that under Article IV they take an oath acknowledging they are "bound... to support this Constitution." More important, it reminds them that this is a nondelegable responsibility that can't merely be pawned off to the judicial branch. Members of Congress cannot take this oath in good faith if they neither know nor care much about the Constitution's foundational concept of limited and enumerated powers.

Several statements by congressional supporters of health-care reform have revealed a disdain for this foundational feature of our constitutional architecture. The idea that there are limits on congressional power, or that members of Congress have a responsibility to ensure such limits aren't exceeded, is apparently a revelation for some. In an August 2010 town-hall meeting packed with Tea Partiers, for example, Democratic Congressman Phil Hare of Illinois responded to a question about the constitutionality of health-care reform by declaring, "I don't worry about the Constitution on this to be honest." He was later caught on camera saying that his constituents' constitutional concerns were "silly stuff." Likewise, Democratic Congressman Henry Waxman of California – the former chair of the powerful Energy and Commerce

Committee that played a large role in writing health-care reform – declared that "[w]hether [Obamacare] is constitutional or not is going to be whether the Supreme Court says it is." Even former House Speaker Nancy Pelosi indicated disbelief that anyone would question the constitutional power of Congress to force individuals to buy a private product. When asked by a CNSNews.com reporter, "Where specifically does the Constitution grant Congress the authority to enact an individual health insurance mandate?" Pelosi replied, "Are you serious? Are you serious?" When the reporter responded, "Yes, yes I am," she shook her head and turned to another reporter. Later, Pelosi's spokesman defended her response, saying, "You can put this on the record. That is not a serious question."

Although it is true that the Supreme Court has the last word on the constitutionality of federal laws, it's a grave mistake for ordinary Americans – much less members of Congress who take the oath to uphold and defend the Constitution – to think the Supreme Court has the only word in such matters. Justice Anthony Kennedy's concurring opinion in *United States v. Lopez* put it this way: "[I]t would be mistaken and mischievous for the political branches to forget that the sworn obligation to preserve and protect the Constitution in maintaining the federal balance is their own in the first and primary instance. . . . The political branches of the Government must fulfill this grave constitutional obligation if democratic liberty and the federalism that secures it are to endure."

If the Constitution is going to survive, every one of the people's representatives – from all branches of government – must be vigilant about upholding it. Passing the constitutional buck to the Supreme Court is both cowardly and deceptive, undermining the role of the political branches and ultimately, their accountability to the American people. When citizens become concerned about Congress exceeding its constitutional powers – as has been the case with health-care reform – they understandably direct those concerns to their elected representatives who are, by definition, politically accountable for their actions. But when these representatives respond to the people's concerns with the equivalent of "that's not my concern, take it to the Supreme Court," the balance of powers is thrown off to a dangerous degree. If the oath of office is to mean anything more than reading one's grocery list, members of Congress, as well as the president, must take greater responsibility in understanding, preserving, and defending the Constitution.

In addition to forcing Congress to go through the motion of articulating the constitutional basis for its assertions of authority, the reform may also positively affect future constitutional challenges to federal laws. For example, because the health-care reform law didn't have to abide by this new rule, the Obama administration has been free, in the context of litigation challenging the act's constitutionality, to cite an ever-changing array of constitutional power sources to justify the law, including the power to tax, to regulate interstate commerce, and the Necessary and Proper Clause. If the health-reform law were enacted today, by contrast, the new rule would ensure that there's a fixed and unambiguous articulation of the constitutional powers relied on, which could be constructive in courts' constitutional analysis.

These initial, originalism inspired reforms implemented by the Tea Party are encouraging. They reflect the movement's belief that the best way to honor and defend the Constitution is to interpret it in a manner consistent with the meaning ascribed by those who ratified it. The debate between originalism and living constitutionalism isn't just a debate of concern to lawyers and political ideologues. It's a debate that has far-reaching implications for the lives of every American. And the choice between the two couldn't be starker: either the written Constitution has a fixed meaning or it doesn't. If it doesn't, why have a written Constitution at all? Equally important, why would the founders have felt the need to provide a mechanism for amendments, in Article V, if the Constitution could be legitimately changed through mere reinterpretation by a majority of the Supreme Court? If we aspire to be a nation of laws, not men, then originalism represents the best method to achieve this goal.

Living constitutionalism, at its heart, elevates judges over the people, subjective values over objective rules, and fluidity over stability. We would do well to remember the words of George Washington at his farewell address: "If in the opinion of the people the distribution or modification of the constitutional powers be in any particular wrong, let it be corrected by amendment in the way which the Constitution designates, but let there be no change by usurpation; for though this in the one instance may be the instrument of good, it is the customary weapon by which free governments are destroyed."

☆ 5 ☆

Looking Forward

THE TEA PARTY DEFIES DEFINITION BECAUSE IT'S NOT a political party in the classic sense. A more apt characterization of the Tea Party would be that of an antiparty, a loose conglomeration of individuals coalescing around certain principles, challenging existing political parties to embrace them. The movement has no formal, centralized decision-making authority that dictates talking points or policy positions to its members. Each Tea Party group has sprung up from local grass roots, developing its own sense of priorities and methods of influencing local elections. But it would be a mistake to assume that the Tea Party's decentralization translates into a lack of definable principles. Despite its disperse nature, as this book has shown, Tea Party groups share a belief in three core principles – limited government, U.S. sovereignty, and constitutional originalism – that animate their position on the most contentious issues of the day. More than anything else, these principles define the Tea Party movement, not any unified logo, slogan, office, or central organizing committee. And the common thread running through all three principles is that they're derived from the U.S. Constitution itself.

The Tea Party's future will be largely determined by whether the majority of Americans – most important, political independents – agree that these principles are both important and under serious threat. The midterm elections of November 2010 suggested that these principles are resonating, but the biggest test will come with the presidential and congressional elections in 2012. The emergence of a presidential contender with significant Tea Party support, for example, could provide the barometer by which to gauge the depth and breadth of Americans' embrace of these constitutional principles.

Regardless of the 2012 elections, however, the Tea Party movement has provided a fascinating example of the likely future of grassroots American political movements. It's precisely the Tea Party's loose structure and outsider political status that seems to be its greatest long-term strength. The mainstream media seems obsessed with speculating on such things as the following: How can the Tea Party survive without a leader? Why are there so many competing Tea Party groups, including Tea Party Nation, Club for Growth, Tea Party Express, Tea Party 365, Tea Party Patriots, and so on? Will the Tea Party hurt the Republican Party by splitting conservative votes? How can the Tea Party movement be sustained without the support of party machinery and fund-raising mechanisms? But these perceived weaknesses aren't really weaknesses if the movement's goal is the long-term influence of issues rather than the formation of a competing political party – in other words, if the emphasis is on the Tea Party *movement* rather than the Tea *Party*.

In this respect, the Tea Party movement has been analogized to a starfish, invoking a metaphor used in Ori Brafman and Rod Beckstrom's best-selling management book *The Starfish and the Spider: The Unstoppable Power of Leaderless Organizations*. Pursuant to this metaphor, businesses are classified as either spiders or starfish. The former – spiders – are traditional, centralized businesses with a powerful and identifiable head. Crush the head and you debilitate the entire organization. Starfish organizations, by contrast, lack a centralized head and consequently are less vulnerable to attack. Cut off any part of a starfish, and not only will the organism continue to live but also its excised portions can grow back.

The Tea Party is a starfish organization because it has no central head that controls it. Its numerous local groups act like starfish legs, moving in separate directions, yet working in concert and propelling the organism forward. Although there are numerous national Tea Party groups competing for attention, none has emerged as dominant, and there seems to be little interest among rank-and-file Tea Partiers to consolidate or appoint a leader anytime soon. The movement itself is what seems to matter, an organism bound by a common core of principles, happily uncontrolled by central organization.

The Tea Party movement is also unique for its Internet-based open-source mentality, a Wikipedia-like endeavor in which anyone can contribute and no one dominates or dictates. It's really more of a network than an organization per se, a loosely united group of individuals who share a common ideology. In this respect, the Tea Party movement's closest analogues would be the liberal group MoveOn.org and perhaps even al-Qaeda, none of which relies heavily on central leadership but instead represents a collective will – a passion for certain issues.

These sorts of open-source, starfishlike organizations are becoming increasingly common and easy to organize in the Internet age. As law professor Glenn Reynolds pointed out in an April 2009 *Wall Street Journal* op-ed, the Tea Party has been remarkably successful at using modern technology and social media such as Facebook, Twitter, e-mail, and blogs to coordinate and disseminate information about rallies and other events. This technology, Reynolds observes, allows starfishlike groups of people to organize and coordinate themselves, without the need for a formal structure such as a political party or labor union. It also allows the Tea Party to adapt quickly to its environment and membership, responding to local issues and elections in ways that larger, more centralized organizations cannot. Indeed, the Tea Party movement is remarkable for its dynamic back-and-forth dialogue among and between small local Tea Party groups, which enables a constant edit of strategy and position when faced with new developments.

In contrast to the old-school Democrat and Republican Parties – in which the whole party moves in relative lockstep and suffers when leaders are discredited or unpopular – the Tea Party movement is relatively impervious to centralized attack or scandal. This could change in 2012, if the Tea Party movement unifies around a single presidential contender. The mere perception of a Tea Party presidential candidate could, in fact, create spiderlike vulnerability. If a Tea Party presidential candidate subsequently said or did something wildly unpopular with the American people, the questions would become, How would the Tea Party react? Would it do what typical political parties tend to do, circling the wagons to protect their leader at all costs? Or would it join the American public in its condemnation or disapproval of the leader's actions? These are difficult questions to answer in the abstract, without knowing the precise reasons behind a candidate's unpopularity. But if the Tea Party's actions thus far are any indication, it seems reasonable to conclude that the movement would react quite differently from the established Republican or Democrat Parties and support principles over any specific candidate.

The Tea Party movement has evidenced a ruthless fidelity to principles, preferring candidates who espouse those principles over candidates who are more electable. This was evident in the November 2010 U.S. Senate elections, in which Tea Party supporters backed unsuccessful candidates such as Christine O'Donnell in Delaware and Joe Miller in Alaska over better-financed, better-known Republicans. The preference for principles over electability proved more successful with dark-horse candidates such as Rand Paul in Kentucky and Mike Lee in Utah, both of whom pulled upsets to defeat establishment Republicans and go on to win the general election. Tea Party opposition in the 2012 elections to incumbent establishment Republican candidates such as Senators Richard Luger of Indiana and Olympia Snowe of Maine similarly suggest an elevation of principles over people, or even over electoral victory.

The Tea Party's apparent willingness to oppose either Democrats or Republicans who don't share its principles enables more effective influence over issues. By single-mindedly focusing on principles rather than politics, the Tea Party forces all candidates, of whatever political stripe, to address and articulate a position on Tea Party principles. Moreover, it reminds all candidates that there's a formidable block of independent voters who won't blindly pull the voting lever on the basis of the presence of a *D* or *R* after their name. This gives candidates the incentive to focus on issues rather than smear tactics, reiterating that the people are their elected representatives' masters, not the other way around. Indeed, this was the explicit message that organizers of a Chicago Tea Party rally gave to Republican National Committee Chair Michael Steele, whose request to address the group was declined on the basis that "[t]his is an opportunity for Americans to speak, and elected officials to listen, not the other way around."

The Tea Party's principles undoubtedly have greater resonance among modern conservatives than modern liberals or progressives. Tea Party candidates accordingly typically run as Republican, not third-party, candidates. This doesn't mean that the Tea Party is just a Republican spin-off or subset, although it does mean the Tea Party has wisely eschewed the model of an independent political party akin to Ross Perot's Reform Party or the Libertarian Party. The political calculation made by the Tea Party movement is that it can more readily implement its principles and affect issues by reforming existing political parties from within, not competing with them from without. Because limited government, U.S. sovereignty, and constitutional originalism historically have been embraced by more conservatives than liberals, it should come as no surprise that Tea Partiers have chosen to infiltrate the Republican rather than the Democrat Party. As Tea Partiers Dick Armey and Matt Kibbe observed in an August 2010 *Wall Street Journal* op-ed, "The tea party movement is not seeking a junior partnership with the Republican Party, but a hostile takeover of it."

Polling data confirm this migration pattern. An extensive poll based on political typology released by the Pew Research Center in May 2011 revealed that 72 percent of Americans who are "staunch conservatives" and 44 percent of "libertarians" support the Tea Party. The same poll showed that the vast majority of both "Main Street Republicans" (57 percent) and "New Coalition Democrats" (58 percent) have "no opinion" on the Tea Party. By contrast, 67 percent of "solid liberals" disagree with the Tea Party. What these polling data suggest is that those who consider themselves conservative – at least economically conservative – are much more likely to support the Tea Party than those who are liberal.

But notice that the emphasis of the Tea Party movement is decidedly economic and constitutional in nature. The principles of limited government, U.S. sovereignty, and constitutional originalism are undoubtedly "conservative" principles in modern lingo – although ironically they are best described as classical liberalism, a political philosophy widely embraced at the time of the country's founding. These conservative principles aren't the same as the social conservatism that has dominated the conservative movement for the past thirty years. The emphasis of Tea Party conservatism is economic and constitutional, not social. Indeed, one of the fascinating aspects of the Tea Party movement is its assiduous avoidance of most culture-war issues such as gay marriage and abortion. Although some try to characterize the Tea Party's desire to reign in illegal immigration as driven by racism – and thus brand it a culture-war issue – as we've seen, the movement's interest is based on a defense of U.S. sovereignty, one of the movement's three core principles.

Social issues such as abortion or gay marriage, by contrast, have an indirect relationship to both the principle of limited government and constitutional originalism, yet the Tea Party's attitude toward them is best characterized as something between ambivalence and lukewarm support. A June

2010 poll by the *Wall Street Journal* and NBC News found that only 2 percent of self-identified Tea Partiers considered social issues a top priority. Indeed, the overwhelming majority of Tea Partiers are probably best described as moderate on social issues. A *New York Times* and CBS News poll from April 2010, for example, indicated that 57 percent of self-identified Tea Partiers think gay couples should be allowed to either legally marry (16 percent) or enter civil unions (41 percent). The same poll showed that 65 percent of Tea Partiers also support abortion, thinking it should be either "generally available" (20 percent) or "available but under stricter limits" (45 percent). Indeed, there is less than a 10 percentage point gap separating Tea Partiers' and non–Tea Partiers' support of both gay marriage and abortion, the only notable difference being one of degree: Tea Partiers prefer civil unions for gay couples, whereas non–Tea Partiers prefer gay marriage. And regarding abortion, Tea Partiers prefer some limits on abortion, whereas non–Tea Partiers prefer that it be "generally available."

When the Tea Party does evince interest in social issues, it's because the issue implicates the principles of limited government or constitutional originalism. For example, the April 2010 *New York Times* and CBS News poll just referenced revealed that the majority of Tea Partiers (53 percent) think the Supreme Court's landmark abortion decision, *Roe v. Wade*, is a "bad thing," compared to only about a third (34 percent) of non–Tea Partiers. Although one could crudely conclude that labeling *Roe* a "bad thing" means the Tea Partiers want to make abortions illegal again, a closer inspection of the poll numbers shows this to be untrue. Less than a third of Tea Partiers (32 percent) think abortion "should not be permitted," and the remaining two-thirds think it should either be "generally available" or "available but with limits."

Opposition to *Roe*, therefore, must have something to do with the *Roe* decision itself, not with abortion. Many constitutional originalists oppose *Roe v. Wade* not because of any moral assessment of abortion, but because the Constitution says nothing about it. They oppose the concepts of substantive due process and privacy on which *Roe* was intellectually grounded – concepts they consider inconsistent with the meaning of constitutional text and the context in which it was adopted. As such, these originalists believe the question of abortion is best left to the democratic process in each state legislature and should not be constitutionalized by an unelected Supreme Court.

Tea Party agnosticism about most social issues is also evident in the Contract from America, a document that – in typical Tea Party style – was conceived by a lawyer who supported the Tea Party and then solicited input from fellow Tea Partiers regarding the most important things they wanted Congress to accomplish after the November 2010 elections. After developing a list of the top twenty-one items, Tea Partiers' voted to narrow their priorities to a top ten list. The ten items that received the most support from Tea Partiers, in descending order of support, included protecting the Constitution (82.03 percent); rejecting cap-and-trade (72.20 percent); demanding a balanced budget (69.69 percent); enacting fundamental tax reform (64.90 percent); restoring fiscal responsibility and constitutionally limited government in Washington (63.37 percent); defunding, repealing, and replacing government-run health care (56.39 percent); passing an "all of the above" energy policy (allowing exploration of domestic reserves; 55.51 percent); stopping the pork (55.47 percent); and stopping the tax hikes (53.38 percent). Not a single one of the items in the Contract from America relates to culture-war-type issues. Each directly relates to the three principles discussed in this book – limited government, U.S. sovereignty, and constitutional originalism.

Tea Party opponents have also tried to make much out of a supposed link between the Tea Party and Christian evangelism. There is tremendous pressure to discredit the Tea Party movement by drawing this linkage, as doing so would imply that Tea Partiers represent some sort of Trojan horse of social conservatism. It's as though some believe Tea Partiers are just pretending to coalesce around limited government, U.S. sovereignty, and constitutional originalism because those principles sound good to ordinary Americans – whereas in reality, Tea Partiers secretly want to outlaw abortion, stop gay marriage, and harbor secret racist tendencies (which explains why they disapprove of President Obama). All the Tea Partiers' talk about abstract economic and constitutional principles is just a very clever ruse to implement unadvertised discriminatory desires.

Although the polling data have shown that a minority of Tea Partiers are indeed social conservatives, the vast majority of them clearly are not. A Pew Research Center poll released in February 2011 indicated that 42 percent of individuals who agree with the Tea Party also agree with the conservative Christian movement. One would think from this statistic that this proves the Tea Party movement comprises principally social conservatives who want to ban abortion and outlaw gay marriage – and indeed this is how the media generally reported the results of the Pew poll. Yet the truth is that the vast majority of Tea Party supporters in the Pew poll – 57 percent to be exact – said they either disagreed with the conservative Christian movement (11 percent) or had no opinion or had never heard of it (46 percent). Moreover, there was little acknowledgement in the mainstream media that merely agreeing with the conservative Christian movement doesn't automatically translate into political opposition to social issues such as gay marriage or abortion. The far-too-simplistic headline was simply this: there are a lot of Tea Partiers who support the conservative Christian movement, so this must mean that the Tea Party itself is a conservative Christian movement. The fact that the vast majority of self-identified Tea Partiers either didn't care about the conservative Christian movement or opposed it was conveniently disregarded.

The truth is that the Tea Party movement is a large umbrella, encompassing a diverse array of Americans from across the political spectrum, including somewhere between 5 percent and 10 percent of whom self-identify as Democrats. Most consider themselves conservative, but their conservatism is decidedly economic and libertarian in tone, emphasizing smaller government and greater individual liberty and responsibility. Social issues such as gay marriage and abortion, although they may be important to some individuals, are clearly not an agenda item of the Tea Party movement itself. Indeed, if the Tea Party movement had to be summed up in a very simple way, it would be best described as a fiscally conservative, socially moderate movement. Because most Americans would probably describe themselves this way, it becomes apparent why progressives and liberals have invested so much time and energy into trying to discredit the Tea Party as a bunch of racist, homophobic, xenophobic, sexist zealots who want to turn back the clock to 1789. As this book has shown, nothing could be further from the truth.

The Tea Party is threatening precisely because it has tremendous potential to capture broad support among

Americans. Most Americans believe in limited government, American exceptionalism, interpretation of the Constitution according to its original meaning, and defending American sovereignty. They want their government to facilitate security, free enterprise, individual responsibility, and liberty. They aren't looking for a nanny state to assist them from cradle to grave. The extreme positions of progressives and social conservatives – both of which seek to control individual choices for various paternalistic ends – just don't resonate with most Americans; they never have, and hopefully never will. The Tea Party movement is a spontaneous, grassroots revolt against these extremes and a reassertion of the uniquely American values of limited government, U.S. sovereignty, and constitutional originalism.

The 2012 elections will offer a fascinating glimpse into the future of the Tea Party movement. The emergence of a Tea Party presidential candidate, the success of Tea Party candidates in various national and state elections, and the ability of the Tea Party itself to stay on message will portend the Tea Party's continuing influence on issues and American politics. A December 2010 Rasmussen poll indicated that a plurality of Americans (41 percent) expect the Tea Party to play a greater role in the 2012 elections than in 2010. Only 21 percent believe that its role will be smaller.

Equally important, between now and the 2012 elections, Tea Party candidates' ability to continue upsetting the apple cart – to enact meaningful policy changes consistent with Tea Party principles – will significantly influence the movement's future. Will successful Tea Party candidates be able to change politics as usual? Will they be able to reign in runaway deficits and spending? Early actions – such as requiring bills to state their constitutional power source; publishing bills several days before voting on them; attempting to alter and defund Obamacare; and being willing to fight over long-term federal budget cuts, including entitlements – suggests that Tea Party members are at least trying to fulfill their electoral promises but will face opposition by Democrats and establishment Republicans.

But an inability to change conventional politics won't harm the Tea Party movement before the 2012 elections. What will likely matter most, in the eyes of Tea Partiers, is that their elected representatives visibly and persistently try to implement changes consistent with Tea Party principles. If anything, an initial failure by Tea Partiers to achieve their goals – at least when the votes are close – will only fuel the flames, encouraging Tea Partiers to work harder to vote the "bums" out of office and replace them with Tea Party candidates. A December 2010 Rasmussen poll found that an astonishing 77 percent of Tea Partiers think that elected Tea Party candidates will remain true to their beliefs. Such confidence in elected officials is relatively unheard of these days, which reveals an intensity of conviction that bodes well for long-term Tea Party success.

Despite all the obstacles laid in its path – all of the name-calling, fear mongering, misrepresentation, and marginalization – the Tea Party movement seems poised to impact the American political landscape in significant ways. It's helping change the way we view and organize effective political movements, the way we view and educate ourselves about the Constitution, and even the way we define the word *conservative*. The Tea Party's brand of conservatism – a unique blend of fidelity to limited government, constitutional originalism, and defense of sovereignty, blended with a laissez-faire attitude toward markets and morals – transcends race, religion, age, and economic status. Tea Partiers value government for limited purposes but value individuals for all others. This is not just the essence of the Tea Party; it's the essence of America.

Index

233